INTRODUCTION

by the Editor

Welcome. How many times, I wonder, have you sat in a doctor's or dentist's waiting-room leafing through a pile of unreadable crappy old magazines and thought to yourself; "I wish, oh how I wish, all these unreadable crappy old magazines could be conveniently packaged up into one single completely unreadable crappy old magazine"?

Exactly. But nevertheless, this is the magazine for **you**. Hundreds of pages of Parish Newsletters, American Express Luggage Invitations, True Farm Confessions, and Specification Charts For Men Who Have Difficulty Telling The Difference Between Their Car And Their Dong.

We've scoured the Reader's Digest for rare articles not about either Cancer or Heroism. We spent ten long minutes reading every issue of the *Sun* since 1968 in our quest for the Legendary News Item. And we've included them all. Or not, as the case may be.

But this is not merely a parade of cruel lampoons. For within this lovely compendium — as much a Work of Art as it is a pile of steamies — ye can make your fortune. For here within, my fair friend, ye will find the clues that may lead you to the fabulous

I am not the editor, I am not Spock

Golden Brain. Tis worth thousandes of poundes and tis buried somewhere within Great Britain, an exacte and hideouse scale modele of Reaganne's tinie thinkinge organne. No bullshitte. Look ye well, O Hunter, and Dame Fortune be with you, me old cockalorum, but remembere:

*The best of men is only
a man at best
So if you can't find it tough tittie.*

Yours expectorantly,

N.B. The Golden Brain Competition is open to members of the *Spitting Image* team, their relatives, brain modellers, map-readers and hole-diggers. Offer closes Christmas 1986. Please do not piddle in the lift.

FOREWORD

by Susan Hampshire

```
Lid£
EgdjLkerZdsjkewy£%& LesFol
Cm, £%% Tg=Bwgl.+ A&(Tgl+cfgl
LesFol+Kgl?V
+Kooigio% EgdjLkerZdsjkewy
Tg=Bwgl.+ A&(Tgl+cfg +Kgl?V
ldifriweuim, difriweuim,
'Ert klertiOf +Kooigi Ger
```
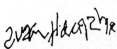

D1138105

BOOK

CONTENTS

ERRATUM

During the production of this book a number of unfortunate errors have been made. The publishers would like to draw the reader's attention to the following corrections to the text:

Page 1 Paragraph 3 Line 22
No mention of the King and Queen of Sweden is implied by this statement. The King and Queen of Sweden are not practicing chiropodists nor have they at any time required their bodies to be used for ritual sacrifice.

Page 17 Paragraph 118 Line 12
Mr Clive Sinclair is not as is implied by this sentence a small grey stain often appearing on the surface of ceramic work areas. He is in fact Chairman of Sinclair Industries and is in no way connected with the *'Ritual Animals For Slaughter Society of Ormskirk'*.

Page 42 Paragraph 2
Add at the foot of this paragraph the phrase: 'Remove your underwear completely and rub cream cheese over your entire body having first informed the librarian of your intentions.

Page 59 Paragraph 6 Line 20
This sentence should read as it appears in the page and under no circumstances should it be amended to the phrase: 'Crushing the hamster lightly between thumb and forefinger until you feel the cranium crack under the pressure. Use an electric vacuum cleaner to remove the pieces.'

Page 73
should read page 79.

Page 104
'Sexual Foreplay Techniques For The Liberated' This page now appears in the book *'Looking After Your Terranium'* by Maxwell and Maxwell.

Page 1
"Erratum" should read "Errati"
"Errati" should read "Errata"

PUBLISHER'S WASHING INSTRUCTIONS

Should the book be heavily stained or have deep soiling we recommend you buy another one.

If stains persist consult your doctor, or seal off the flow with a rubber band.

For light stains the book may be washed in luke warm soapy water. This is GUARANTEED to ruin it. Treat as for deep soiling above.

Wash separately. Each page should be removed from the spine and carefully scrubbed before soaking in biological detergent. This should remove all traces of smut, foul language, ink etc.

dry flat or iron

DO NOT bleach

DO NOT spin dry

DO NOT know what this means

HEADLINERS

A blast from the past. Baron Von Reibnitz arrives at the Church to give away his daughter to Prince Michael of Kent.

Ronnie Reagan ready to negotiate with the Chinese.

Roger Moore arrives in a party mood.

Denis finds a small speck of water in his drink.

Det. Sergeant Dimbleby enjoys the party from a distance.

Eric Heffer proving that Bernard Manning isn't the only fat git who can stand up and tell jokes.

Roger Moore hopping mad at our photographer.

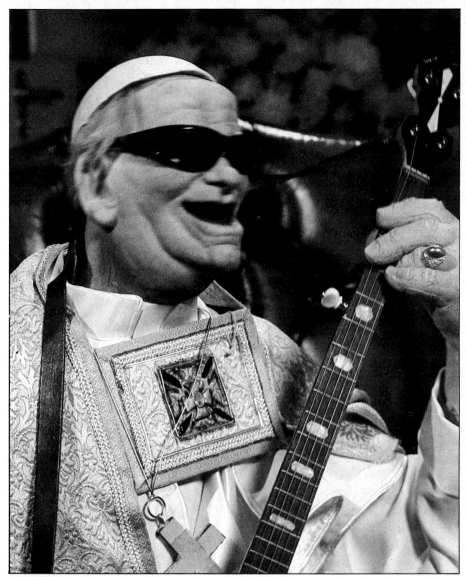

"I got rhythm".

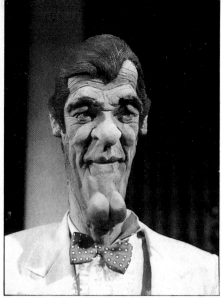

Roger Moore swoons with horror on being told the news.

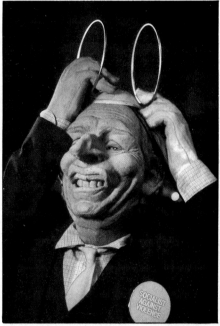

Labour party leader Whatshisname goes after the Mickey Mouse vote.

Rupert Murdoch assures Prince Philip that his paper always gets its facts right.

A radiant Christina Onassis – is there a new man in her life?

Scoreline

for friends, love, marriage – you get the picture

Phil and Nancy – engaged

Nancy says: "I joined SCORELINE because my bedroom hasn't seen any action since the Alamo. I met a lot of nice sincere guys. And then I met Phil. He's incredible. I've never done it without a lasso before."

Bob and Enoch – married

Enoch says: "I signed up with SCORELINE for companionship, conversation and a bit of S & M. Unfortunately, they'd run out of girls again, so I met Bob. One thing led to another, and we now have three children."

WHO JOINS SCORELINE?

Hundreds of people all over the country have joined Scoreline, as a way of meeting new friends, making lasting relationships, enjoying the warmth of another personality . . . do we have to spell it out?

ALL KINDS OF PEOPLE USE SCORELINE

Doctors, Dentists, Lawyers, Judges, Roman Catholic Priests – Even Nuns are on our books. So don't feel shy about Scoreline. We know exactly what you're after.

HOW DOES SCORELINE WORK?

We put your completed Questionnaire straight into the bin and pick out a name from a hat. Then it's all up to you.

IS SCORELINE SUCCESSFUL?

It is for us.

CONFIDENTIAL **FREE**

SCORELINE COMPUTER TEST
Tick the following:

4. Do you consider yourself:
- ☐ Shy.
- ☐ Extrovert.
- ☐ Outdoor Type.
- ☐ In need of a bit of Hokey Pokey, to be honest.

2. Indicate your preferences for the following interests.
- ☐ Pop Music.
- ☐ Opera.
- ☐ Theatre.
- ☐ Art.
- ☐ Literature.
- ☐ Leg-Over.

I am over seventeen and would like you to send me completely free details of Scoreline's Dating Service (£3,590.45p) and also a brochure outlining the advantages of Scoreline's 'Brytawindow Double Glazing'. And I don't mind if a salesman calls at my home any evening. I am also very interested in a complete set of the Scoreline Encyclopaedia Anglica (29 volumes).

NAME_____

ADDRESS_____

3. Which of the below do you find attractive.
- ☐ A
- ☐ B

A   B

We will send you a detailed profile of your ideal partner, or a set of saucepans, depending on preference.

For friends, love, marriage and yes, all right, that as well.

Scoreline

32

The Puzzler

TELL ME WHY
Here's a toughie to start with: why is there a picture of a semi-naked woman on the cover of this magazine?

34 SOUTH AFRICAN CROSSWORD

35

BY CUTTING OUT THESE LETTERS AND STICKING THEM ONTO YOUR EXISTING SET, YOU CAN PLAY WELSH SCRABBLE©

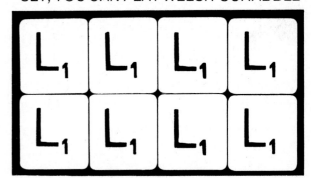

36 WORD GAME

HOW MANY WORDS CAN YOU MAKE OUT OF THE RANDOM LETTERS BELOW?

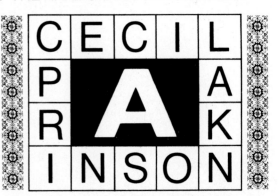

ANSWER

Piraña, Cecil, Likes, Personal, Sec, Sara, Spankie, Pankie, In, Car, Park, Like, An, Oik, Slap, Arse, Lick, Niples, Snap, Nicks, Rip, San, Crap, On, Ankles, Aar, Real, Ace, Cack, Oaar, Clean, Crack, No, Lice, So, Slip, In, Pan, Oaark, Orka, Ikra, Irpa, Arpa, Moi, Ale, Aik, Kroom, Ik, Nice, Kip, Porkie, Penis, Like, a, Pink, Icicle, Oa, Aa, Oink, Ork, Arp, Aark, Rasp, Arise, Soak, Nose, In, Persil, Rinse, Plonker, In, Lake, Clean, Prick, On, Pencil, Case, Slink, In, Sara, Is, Sick, No, Cap, Parkie, Opens, Parcel, O, Cripes, A, Son, I, Can, Lose, Pension, So, Parkinson, In, Sack, And, Then, He, Gets, His, Old, Job, Back, From, Thatcher, Which, Is, Cheating, But, Who, Cares, Were, The, Government, So, Sod, You.

COSMOPOLITAN

Octoberleutnant

October 1985 • 80p

THE NORMAN ST. JOHN STEVAS OUT-OF-WORK-OUT

FIVE NEW ORGASMS TO BE WON! plus

Why you'll never be a lone!

STAYING INDEPENDENT TO PLEASE YOUR MAN

HOW GULLIBLE ARE YOU? Send £5 for our searching questionnaire plus **Your problems made up** and **The new "Eat Less" diet**

YOUR CLITIS
WHERE IS IT REALLY?

The Clitis – one of the great mysteries of the female body. Where is it? What is it? And what do the modern couple do with it once they find it. George Fraud, an eminent London doctor (of Law) tackles these modern problems.

In this modern age, populated with modern men and modern women, with their modern cars and really modern kitchens, many of the taboos of yester year have disappeared completely. The modern man is as happy discussing tampons, menstrual cycles, inverted nipples, and multiple orgasms, as he is football. Understains, however, remains taboo.

But how does the modern man view the clitis? Well, as in any discussion where you're paid by the word, the answer isn't simple. Perhaps the major change from 50 years ago is in the question that the male asks; the shift has been from 'What is it?' to 'Where the bloody hell is it?' In my extensive research, conducted last Saturday afternoon, I have come to the conclusion that the clitis is located either inside the ear or directly behind the knee. Or it might as well be as far as my wife's concerned.

Perhaps more importantly is the question of what to do with it once located, and the answer is 'Don't ask me – although I imagine it's something sexual'. It is becoming increasingly clear that asking it out for a game of tennis is wasting everybody's time. Now have I answered all the questions? … eh … oh no … eh what is it?

Right. Well quite simply it's a pleasure centre, rather like a sports complex, although much harder to hurdle in.

Finally I was very fortunate a couple of months ago to conduct a frank and forthright interview with Mr Fred Hampson, a retired clitis. I asked him just why are clitises so difficult to find? His answer was both simple and illuminating. 'Well if every time you came out a hundred foot thumb battered you over the head, then I'd imagine that you'd lie pretty low.' Well there you have it, they mystery solved and my new stereo paid for.

Below are some informative diagrams which take up a lot of space.

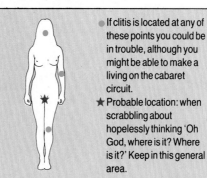

- If clitis is located at any of these points you could be in trouble, although you might be able to make a living on the cabaret circuit.
- ★ Probable location: when scrabbling about hopelessly thinking 'Oh God, where is it? Where is it?' Keep in this general area.

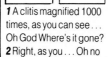

1 A clitis magnified 1000 times, as you can see … Oh God Where's it gone?
2 Right, as you … Oh no
3 Note well the markings on … oh forget it.
4 Aha! Gotcha – there he is – the clitis.

first among sequels

Charles Wentworth, the youngest M.P. in the commons, sipped his gin and tonic and waited for the phone to ring. It did. He picked it up and said in his Old Etonian and Balliol College Oxford educated voice, "Hello". There was a pause. "Hello", came back the Roedean and Swiss Finishing School voice which contained just a hint of her Polish father and poverty stricken Jewish violin playing mother who had fought their way from the ghettoes of Warsaw to become part of the class ridden English Society … where was I? … oh yes … "Hello, Charles, my little under-secretary for Finances" she whispered softly. "Hello, Anne. How's my little Sotheby's Medieval Italian Art expert then?" She laughed scornfully "Ha Ha

▶ 109

No FT...

FINANCIAL TIMES

No thank you.

MADEUPPIES

A new sociological phenomenon has burst upon the scene. No more is the smart talk in Winebars concerned with Yappies or Fogeys. Suddenly everyone is talking about "Lones". Who are they? They are a new group in our style conscious society who are destined to hit the headlines and push Foodies and Yuppies out of the Sunday supplements: – Yes, "Lones" are here, like it or not.

But where do they come from? Trend spotters claim that they are not new at all and the first "Lone" was seen for the first time as long ago as the 1950s. Who knows? The important thing is that they are here and now and you ignore them at your peril. Are you a Lone Ranger? Probably not, but then you may ask how does one tell? One theory says that there is a bit of "Lone" in all of us, another suggests that there are no "Lones" at all. But let's face it, there's no doubt when the genuine article hits town. And it's not just his clothes. There's something about him that says "I'm a Lone Ranger" in a way that you just can't argue about. He's distinctive, special, indescribably "Lone". He stands out from the crowd – Lone and Ranging. So who are they? Oh yes, I've just covered that. This new breed of man, this style-warrior has exploded into the public consciousness with something about which says "I'm a Lone Ranger" in a way that you just can't argue about. Oh dear, I've done that bit already. So "Lone Ranger": – Fact or Fiction? Myth or Reality? Truth or Fantasy? Illusion or . . . some other word? Perhaps we'll never know for sure. But one thing is certain. The Lone Ranger is here to stay. Or is he? Perhaps we shall never know for sure. Oh no, I've done that bit as well. So that just about says it all, doesn't it, about this man of the moment, this nomad in the echelons of class, this something else sort of person who we all have come to know as the Lone Ranger. Or not. I've done my bit (500 words) now it's up to you. Phew.

From the latest style-stunner by Peopling-Tom Peter Statetheobvious "The Lone Ranger Handbook" (SPURIOUS & FEEBLE £12.95)

WHAT LONES WEAR
Black Mask
Stetson
Suede Jacket with Tassels
Holster with silver gun

FAVOURITE LONE NAMES
Lone
Ranger
Kimosabbee

WHO THEIR FRIENDS ARE
Tonto
Silver

WHERE "LONES" HANG OUT
Dodge City
Arizona
The Desert, Generally

WHERE THEY GO FOR THEIR HOLIDAYS
Lones are far too busy righting wrongs to go on holiday

WHERE "LONEYS" GO TO SCHOOL
Marlborough
Eton
Winchester
St Pauls
Dodge City Primary School

"LONEYS" MODEL THEMSELVES ON
The Lone Ranger
Prince Charles
Richard Ingrams

FAVOURITE LONE JOBS
Lawman
Fighter of Evil
Indian Lover

FAVOURITE PHRASES
Hiho Silver
Hello Tonto

FAVOURITE "LONEY" FRIENDS
Beans
Steak
Beans

WHAT "LONEYS" DRINK
Water
Coffee
Cactus Juice

WHAT LONES DO IN THE EVENING
Play the harmonica
Clean their revolvers
Sleep

FAVOURITE LONE BARS
Doc Halliday's "Red Eye" Saloon, Dodge City.
Stringfellows

By Peter State & Anne The Bleeding Obvious

Peter Statetheobvious is a celebrated commentator on style, being Sock Editor of a number of glossy magazines. He is the author of many style best-sellers including the runaway success "The Guppy Handbook", a guide to the Ins and Outs of bright coloured small tropical fish. He is responsible for giving the English Language the Phrase "The Lone Ranger".

COSMOPOLITANS CUT-OUT & KEEP GUIDE TO
CONTRACEPTION

METHOD	FAILURE RATE	EMBARRASSMENT FACTOR	METHOD	FAILURE RATE	EMBARRASSMENT FACTOR
THE PILL.	0-2%	Fairly low. Potential embarrassment when staying with Catholic relatives and trying not to rattle the silver foil. Also having to leave in the middle of film/dinner party/job interview because you've just remembered you forgot to take it. This method can prove very embarrassing to those who have not learned the days of the week.			During insertion, this device has a tendency to catapult across the room. A stable relationship necessary to withstand humiliation induced by this method.
			THE SPONGE	Uncertain	Embarrassing only if your partner asks "Isn't that what I use for washing the car?"
CONDOM (SHEATH, JOHNNY, FRENCH LETTER, RUBBER ETC)	3-6%	High. This is to be expected, given the wide variety of silly names for it. If using this method, it is advisable to be a witty conversationalist to bridge the 15 minute gap in sexual relations while putting it on. No variety of colours or textures will prevent you from looking daft wearing one. Extra embarrassment is experienced if you can't find it afterwards.	INTRA-UTERINE DEVICE (IUD OR COIL)	2-4%	Medium embarrassment factor, caused when the device picks up messages from the space shuttle during intercourse.
			SPERMICIDES (FOAMS, JELLIES, CREAMS)	10-14%	High. For obvious reasons (who wants to make love to a gateau?).
			COITUS INTERRUPTUS	10-40%	Post-coital embarrassment, experienced when going to the laundry.
THE DIAPHRAGM (CAP)	3-12%	High. When not in use, is likely to fall out of handbag. When in use, is likely to fall out of body.	RHYTHM METHOD	High	High, (again, after intercourse) when asked to pay child maintenance.

◆ Airports

PORT STANLEY International Airport:

Bookings	Falklands 1
Departure lounge	Falklands 1
VIP lounge	Falklands 1
Duty Free	Falklands 1
Flight Control	Falklands 1
Plane	Falklands 1
Pilot	Falklands 1
Pilot's Mum	Falklands 1
Pilot's Friend	Falklands 1
Pilot's Other Friend	Falklands 1
Pilot's Other Other Friend	Falklands 1
Pilot's Clinic	Falklands 1

◆ British Secret Service

Colin Evans Gutter Maintenance Specialist .... Falklands 1

◆ Discotheques & Dance Halls

(SEE ALSO: NIGHTCLUBS)

DISCOTHEQUE
5 GOOSE GREEN
FALKLANDS 1

SMART DRESS –
NO COWS   **8 TIL LATE**

◆ Emergency Services

Fire	9
Police	9
Ambulance	9
Sheep	9

◆ Funeral Services

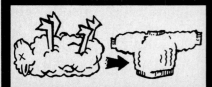

Morton's Sheep Undertakers

Have your loved one knitted
as a memorial jumper

Falklands 1

◆ Hairdressers

A Pun Worse Than The Rest	Falklands 1
A Cut Above The Usual Pun	Falklands 1
A Snip Above The Pun	Falklands 1
A Hair's Breadth Away From Being The Worst Possible Pun	Falklands 1

Chez Pretentious Pun	Falklands 1
On The Fringe Of Being A Pun	Falklands 1
A Pun Ahead	Falklands 1
The Pun's Edge	Falklands 1

◆ Gloria Hunnifords

(SEE: TERRY WOGANS)

◆ Massage

Daisie's Sauna and Massage
Visit-ing Sheep Massage

For a relaxing and unhurried massage by attractive and friendly sheep, phone: **FALKLANDS 1**

Credit Cards Welcome

◆ Menswear

IN GEAR

Wind-cheaters – Anoraks-Large
Bri-Nylon range – *Hand-tailored
Donny Osmond hats*
Velvet jackets – Laurel And Hardy
Shirts – *Hipster jeans (guaranteed
bottom cleavage)*

**5A Goose Green
Falklands 1**

Dickish Clothing for Men

◆ Motoring Associations

ROYAL AUTOMOBILE CLUB

24-HOUR SERVICE AND WAITING TIME

Falklands 1

◆ Sex Shops

◆ Sheep Repairs

**TIBSON'S
Sheep repairs**

Burst or
partially-
exploded
sheep

24-HOUR
SERVICE
FALKLANDS 1

◆ Suicide Agencies

(SEE ALSO: EUTHANASIA ADVISORS)

Exit .... Argentina 554-6777

◆ Terry Wogans

Wogan, T	Falklands 1
Wogan, Terry	Falklands 2
Wogan, Tel	Falklands 3
Wogan, Terrance	Falklands 5

◆ TR7 Owners Clubs

**TR7
OWNERS'
CLUB**

*Meets every Thursday for
comfort, solace and kind words.*

*Why not push your car to one of
our meetings?*

Telephone: Falklands 1

◆ Zebra Re-Tooling

(SEE: SHEEP REPAIRS)

JOY

*5B GOOSE GREEN
FALKLANDS 1*

**VAST
SELECTION OF
LOVE-TOYS**

Including: 1. Sheep-opener   2. French Tickler Gumboots   3. Lamb suspenders   4. Stiletto Hooves   5. Sheep Action-Delay Creme (wool flavoured)   6. Aroused Sheep (Long-playing Album)   7. Sheep Lubricant (mint sauce flavoured)   8. Penguin Whistle (reproduces call of rampant King Penguin)

The Kentucky Fried Chicken Chicken
(Latinus Humourous)

Reputedly discovered at the turn of the century by a Private Sanders in a skip outside the Genetics Experiment Foundation in California. Until this point in his life, Sanders had been an unremarkable young man, save for his ability to whistle "Hello Young Lovers" through a bullet hole in his head. But this breastless, multi-legged fowl inspired Sanders to invest his life savings in a chain. And Sanders would stand on street corners and hit people with it until they gave him some money. He opened a string of shops. The rest is history. Except for this equation: $x(xy)x-/y=3x$, which is algebra.

A full grown bird has been known to sport 180 legs, none of which it uses for walking. This bird is so stupid, that, if it were taught Latin, it would probably decline Respublica as if it were a single noun!

The chicken habitually makes its home 50 yards away from the nearest MacDonalds, or Wimpy. It eats carrots and whitewash, which it regurgitates into small red and white plastic containers. It shits bar-b-que beans. It keeps warm by rolling in bread crumbs and makes its nest in boiling fat. Research suggests that the dead bird gives off toxic fumes which cause outrageous acne and an unnatural desire to wear silly cardboard hats.

The Obvious Fish
(Yumus Yumus)

The Obvious Fish is one of God's "little mistakes", like the lift operator in Drebley's, Manchester.

Although they are believed to be extinct, a shoal of Obvious Fish (collective name a "restaurant") was reported as recently as 1856 by a whaler off Cape Cod: "... *Having thus rendered our harpoon stock to the back of the great leviathan, we made sail for Nantuckkett, whereupon our attentions were arrested by a tumultuous wailing, a pleasant and mellifluous sound, and the decks were beset by deliciously coloured fish, who hurled themselves into our mouths and slithered down to our stomachs. And I hesitate to record, but the devil take my soul if the cries they made didn't sound for all the world like "Eat me! Eat me!". It was the strangest experience of my life – save for the one with the pelican and the cabin boy."* (Captain Elijah K Headstone, his log).

The Swissarmyknifeosaur
(Bogus Jokis)

The Swissarmyknifeosaur roamed the Earth during the Miocene Era which began 260 billion years ago, and lasted all weekend. It was a cold-blooded herbivorous reptile with the ability to open a bottle of pale ale and change a plug with a posidrive screw, many epochs before there was any urgent call so to do. It appealed initially to other dinosaurs, who thought "What a handy thing to have around", until they realised they only ever really got much use out of the penknife and the nail clipper, and it quickly fell out of favour. The dinosaurs ruled when the Earth was in a state of flux, with mountain ranges forming, continents shifting and huge landmasses breaking apart. This must have been very irritating, and they must have wished they'd moved on to a planet which was already furnished, even if it wasn't in quite such a fashionable area. However, after spending every weekend and most evenings for 550 million years, the dinosaurs finally got the place looking pretty much as they wanted except for Wolverhampton. Then, typically, the dinosaurs left, and some slime moved in. Exactly where the Swissarmyknifeosaur and his ilk went, no one is sure, and that's why their mail has never been forwarded.

25-31 May 1967   6d

Thames/LWT
and Channel Four

TV Times

INSIDE

LULU IS BACK!
The wee Scots lass
returns in a new series of
Freeman's Catalogue Adverts

THE SOAP WARS
Who gives a toss?

HE AUDIENCE FIGURE IS RIGHT!
New crass game show
starts on Saturday

PLUS: More Bullshit
from Katie Boyle

The woman who tamed 103-year old Lee Marvin

Dull though she is, would have been infinitely preferable to the bigoted old toad we ended up with.

Bernard Manning returns to ITV* in another season of guest appearances on other people's game shows. He talks here to **Fred Fudge** about something completely unconnected with the program, for some odd reason.

I like this opening paragraph, because it gives me the writer, the opportunity to get in a few snidey digs about the star before he gets a chance to open his mouth. You know the kind of thing: "He was half-an-hour late", "He was bleary-eyed from a night on the town", or whatever. Anyway, I intend to make full use of this little bit of freedom. . .oh bums! I've almost run out of paragraph. Perhaps I can get in a dig or two in the.

"Scabs," said Bernard Manning, stretching his more-than ample sweating frame. There. I managed to get in *two* insults, and that's within the main body of the interview, so already, I'm beginning to make up for lost time on that stupid opening paragraph. "I've always collected scabs", said old Fat Face (another one), "ever since I was a nipper." He smiles, scabbily (and again!) "At first, it was my own scabs, from schoolboy scrapes. Then I got them from friends, as they grew up and started to throw theirs away. In the Navy, I almost doubled my collection after a visit to Tokyo Rose's sauna and relief massage parlour in Bangkok," he said, in a single breath, so I couldn't interrupt him with anymore of my sly remarks. The slobby, fat, pig-like pig! Piggy-wiggy portly obese fat pig. "Now I've got the biggest collection in Europe. Only Arthur Scargill has more than I do. But I keep mine in a box." Dammit, I've run out of article, and I haven't even started my summing-up insults.

*Although he's never actually left, unfortunately.

Thames

7.00 Carry On Up The Rectum

SID JAMES
CHARLES SCREAMER
KENNETH NOSTRILS
DORA BOOBS
LIZ BOOBIES
JULIE BREASTS
FATTY JAQUES
and starring Barbara
Windsor's saggy old bum.

A chance to welcome back yet again, yet again, another batch of the highspots from this specially re-edited version of the other re-edited version based on the films no one ever went to see.

This week – some of the best jokes about bottoms.
DIRECTOR PRATT FALL
PRODUCER WALTER HERZOG
Thames Television

 Be sure to place a regular order

7.30 Coronation Street

Once again, actors from Oldham Rep get the chance of some steady money.

For cast, see Wednesday
PRODUCER BILL KILLSTAR
Grandad TV

8.00 Closedown

(Anglia area only)

8.30 World In Action

This week, the award-winning team investigates the growing unrest on Monday nights at 8.30, when there's only this and *PANORAMA* on the other side.
PRODUCER OXFORD HYPHEN-CAMBRIDGE
Granada TV

9.00 Quincy

JACK KLUGMAN

When police pathologist, Quincy, examines the body of a naked girl, the trouble starts because she's still alive.
Hubert Angry
          Bad Tempered Boss
Sid Reasonable
          Quincy's Chinese Chum
LWT

9.00 'Call My Bluff'. Very good but unfortunately on the other side

10.00 News At Ten

followed by

More bloody news

10.30 Hey Baby – Be Groovy

CRAIG DOUGLAS
ALAN FREEMAN
BILLY J. KRAMER
HANK MARVIN
BOBBY VEE
SIR JOHN GIELGUD

 Karen Beat *(Helen Shapiro)* is on the Pill, wears a mini-skirt and doesn't give a fig what the establishment thinks. Until she meets smooth-talker Ephram Kool *(Simon Dee)* who persuades her to enter a hoola-hoop competition.

Music by The Applejacks With Esther and Abi Ofarim as themselves
PRODUCER JIM "HIP" OLDMAN
DIRECTOR FREE LIBERTY
HTV

12.25 Night Thoughts

Sanctimonious old bint waffles on self - righteously about humility.

followed by

Closedown

Sir John tries free love at 10.30

Griffin learns the facts of life from school leavers.*

WHY ARE YOU SO BADLY DRAWN GRIFFIN?

WHY HASN'T YOUR AD. AGENCY TOLD YOU YOU GIVE EVERYONE THE CREEPS?

WHY HAVEN'T YOU GOT A WILLY?

*But being a banker takes not the blindest bit of notice

Free money

Yes, we get your money absolutely free. And then we spend it any way we damn well please. Designing hideous expensive new credit cards with a hologram of a pigeon on them. Giving our employees 3% mortgages. Buying Ade Edmondson a new yacht.

Free threatening letters for 3 years

Yes, we'll be incredibly rude and difficult to you if you overdraw your account by so much as the price of a Malteser. You're an inconvenient bloody little sod aren't you? Your measly £28 pw doesn't even cover the cost of your free pen-chain pouch. Why you scruffy bastards can't just give us your money and be done with it – but oh no, you want it back again *and* then you winge if it doesn't come with a free leaflet-case. You make us sick. Except that nice Mr. Edmondson, of course.

Free leaflets for life

To start with we offer free leaflets about incredibly dull things like "Probate", "Insuring A Greenhouse" etc. But for only 15½% – 17¼% interest, you can also get free leaflets on "Why Quick Service Counter", "Why We Put Chains On Pens That Don't Work", "Who's The Man Who Sits At The Desk In The Middle And Has To Be Continually Asked To Leave."

I'm too young to know better. Please send me your leaflet "Leaving School And Having My Personal Details Fed To The Police Computer And Anyone Else Who Asks For Them For The Privilege Of Paying You 18¼% Interest"

Name

Address

Natlays Midloyd
The Listening Bank

Scottish Goalkeeping
the five golden rules!

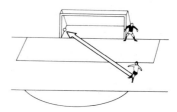

1 BODY BEHIND THE BALL ▼
Keep your body behind the ball to make any save a formality.

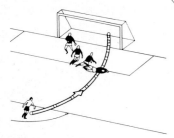

3 ANTICIPATION ▲
All great goalkeepers try to anticipate shots before hand. It will give you more time to collect the ball and will allow you to gather the shot with comfort.

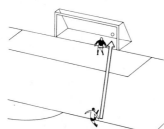

2 CAUTION ►
Many goalkeepers go for balls they can't get and put themselves in great difficulty as a result. By not going for balls you can't reach you make your job much easier.

4 ANGLES ▲
Know your angles, narrow down angles and you will make the goal seem much smaller to any attacking player.

5 SAFETY FIRST ▲
Try and prevent danger when facing a pass back from your own defender. Move to the side of your goal then if he mishits his shot the worst that can happen is you will give away a corner.

Play the DAVIS way

STEVE 'INTERESTING' DAVIS is one of snooker's most flamboyant characters. There's never a dull moment when Steve's around! His crazy antics are legendary amongst snooker players. He's been known to play a whole frame with his bow tie slightly askew. But he's not just a joker, Steve's a pretty good snooker player too! One of his most famous trick shots is called 'THE STEVE DAVIS TRICK SHOT' a name he cheekily coined himself. But that's the kind of guy he is.
Here's how it works . . .

'I strike the cue ball onto the object ball, it hits the baulk cushion, jumps off the table, then it rolls through the door, down the steps, catches the number nineteen bus, picks up my laundry, takes it home, irons my underwear, lays out my clothes neatly in the bottom left hand drawer of my wardrobe, then pops a Marks and Spencer's pie in the microwave, phones up my mum, pays my ACCESS bill, and has a little nap. Then it gets up, a quick shower and catches the bus back to the snooker hall, where it strikes the object ball, cannons into the black, makes a cup of tea and goes in off the pink. If this shot comes off, it can be a real show stopper. But you must remember not to put too much top spin on, otherwise the ball catches the 78 bus by mistake, which is a longer journey and costs 17p more. This is one of the many reasons I'm known as Steve 'Interesting' Davis. The other reason is my comprehensive collection of bus tickets. But that's another story, fans. 'Bye.'

Subbuteo TABLE SWIMMING

Capture all the authentic thrills of international competition in your own living room.

EACH SET CONTAINS

- ● Eight subbuteo© swimmers
- ● Finely detailed Olympic pool
- ● 2 Gallons of chlorinated water
- ● 1 Swimmer being resuscitated
- ● 1 Duncan Goodhew
- ● 1 Sharron Davies with current boyfriend
- ● 8 Dry towels
- ● 2 Wet towels
- ● 1 Cockroach
- ● 3 Verrucas
- ● 2 Cups hot Bovril
- ● 1 Thing found floating in pool

COMING SOON!! TABLE SHOWJUMPING!

Using fingertip control, you can give your swimmers all the skill and speed of professionals.

Breast stroke

Crawl

Butterfly

Backstroke

Flick the swimmer into the pool, flick him all the way to the end, then flick him back again – it's exactly like the real thing!

QUESTION OF SPORT

By David Coleman

Aaaaand welcome back. It really is quite remarkable how popular *"Question of Sport"* actually is. Aaaaand now I have devised a way of capturing all the thrills and excitement of this ever popular TV show in your very own sitting room, with *you* as the question master. First, simply hire, for one evening, six sporting celebrities. Two of which should have squeaky voices. Then buy an Outside Broadcast Unit, with editing facilities. And of course a Quantel console for those "zappy" TV effects. You'll require a lighting crew, a small make-up department, chippies and sparks, scene-shifters, security men (the surlier the better), director/producer (you could do this yourself if you're in the ACTT), production secretaries (the more world weary and embittered the better), at least twelve gays (one closet), catering, an accountant, creative producers, hairdresser, props, researchers, medical unit, question deviser, set builder, production assistants, floor manager (one big fat one should do), a small duplicating office, vision mixer, dubbing suite and crew, 2 buzzers and 7 vee-neck jumpers, and there you have it. You're ready to play *"Question of Sport"* in your own front room. And to get started, here are some questions:

1 WHAT HAPPENED NEXT?
Here's a famous sporting incident, with the action frozen. *WHAT HAPPENED NEXT?*

***ANS:* Yes, it was, of course, the famous '67 crown green bowls championship, where Jim Sibson rolled the jack to start the final.**

2 Here's a famous sporting personality doing something other than what he is famous for.

***ANS:* Yes, it was, of course, Charlie Nicholas scoring for Arsenal.**

My Favourite SPORTING MOMENT

★This week★
JIMMY GREAVES

Well, my favourite sporting moment has got to be the Geoff Hurst hat-trick in the '66 World Cup Final. It was particularly memorable for me, as Hurst got into the side, at my expense, when I was at the very peak of my sporting prowess after which I hit the bottle and went on the slide for five or six years. Yeah, thanks, Geoff, old chum. I've nothing against Geoff, however, you've got to ask 'What is Hursty doing now?' Eh? Is he on the same cushy number what other certain ex-international inside forwards is on? Well, if he is, I've never seen the show. Does he get the same benefits, such as free trips to football matches with a programme thrown in, a decent seat every time, as much half-time Bovril as he can drink absolutely free, a lift home from the Saint without any bothersome petrol money arguments, as other certain nimble-footed, quicksilver goalscorers of yesteryear? No. I don't know what he's doing, to be frank. He's probably sitting in the park slinging bread at the ducks, which is something I only have to do *five* days of the week. So, Geoff, me old china, you may have been the hero of English Football's finest hour, but you're a git, and I'm not. Plus you haven't got a *Spitting Image* sweatshirt, gratis. Nor will you ever have. So stick that in your sports outfitters shop in Bromley and smoke it.

Cheers,
Greavsie

BJORN BORG's TENNIS-KLASSEN

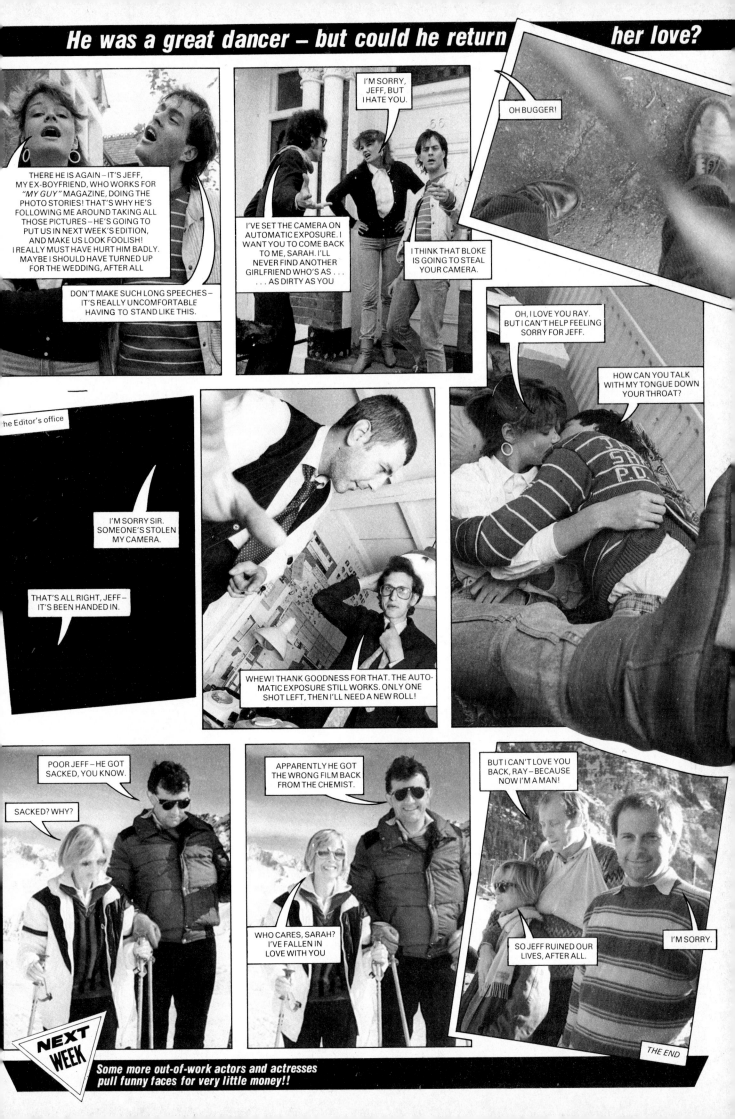

WHICH HOME PERSONAL COMPUTER

Micro boring dull yawn MAGAZINE?

Letters
to the Police computer

TO THE CHAIRMAN
THE NATIONAL COUNCIL FOR CIVIL LIBERTIES

ALPEN
THE BRIDLEWAY
GORING
30th MAY 1985

Dear Sir,

It is with some regret that I write to inform you of my decision to resign from the NCCL. My conscience will not allow me to subscribe to policies which, in too many cases, have become inconsistent and selective.

If having clean air is a fundamental right then we must also defend the rights of those who prefer the nasty stinky type. Again, the right of the individual not to be tortured should not be permitted to stand in the way of those who quite like it.

Above all I question your support of free speech for some and not for others. If it is a basic right then it must also be extended to political parties which would do away with free speech; And also of course to opponents of such parties, to critics of these opponents, to people who would deny a platform to such critics, to those who choose to speak out against such people, and to those, like myself, who don't give a toss what anyone says about anything.

Yours sincerely,

Roland E. Oderant

NEW!!! FROM sinclair RESEARCH

The Sinclair We-haven't-thought-of-it-yet

Yes – if you're a computer user, a car driver, wear a watch or watch TV, you'll need the **Sinclair** © **We-haven't-thought-of-it-yet** © **It's certain to be revolutionary. It's certain to be small.**

TECHNICAL SPECIFICATIONS*
4 MILLION K RAM
4 MILLION K ROM
5 MILLION K RIM
COLOUR Black
TANGLED LEADS 12-ish
WIRES yellow & green, black, red
SQUELCHY RUBBER KEYBOARD
*probably

AVOID DISAPPOINTMENT. When the whatever it is comes out, as usual there won't be nearly enough of them. So order yours now, before we've even started to think about it.
Be one of the first to get this thing hot off the benches. You'll be guaranteed a brand new fully-flawed, fully-non-ready pro-totype in superb white styrofoam packing.

Compact, Powerful and Amazingly Cheap.

Please send me .... SINCLAIR WE-HAVEN'T-THOUGHT-OF-IT-YET© as soon as you think of it.
*I enclose a cheque, which you will not cash until you receive it.
*In return, I will receive: 1 Whatever it is 1 Subscription to
'SINCLAIR WE-HAVEN'T-THOUGHT-OF-IT-YET USER' Magazine.
First chance to purchase Whatever-it-is peripherals the Whatever-it-is will need to function at all.
But mostly I will get thoroughly pissed off wondering when the hell I'm going to get it.

NAME

ADDRESS   ZIP SIZE

sinclair

PICK OF THE CROP

Games Review

Fruit Computers have just issued a new series of computers designed to capture the jokey names market from Apple. Which Home Personal Computer Micro Boring Dull Yawn magazine rates their chances in a series of hands-on tests:

Loganberry

An advanced computer with a name so fruity you can bet as soon as people hear it they'll go "Ho-hum, that sounds like a computer to me alright."

Pun rating:
Poor. Have to rely on "Ram" and "Rom" and other old faithfuls.

damson

Damson

A really nice fruity sounding computer with just the sort of fruity name computer users like.

Pun rating:
Not bad. Good mileage out of "damson in distress" etc.

Mango

A very fruity computer for those who like their computers nice and tangy.

Pun rating:
Fair. Usual "bytes" of the mango, etc.

tinned peach

Tinned Peach

Still a fruity sort of name but with a tinny nuance so you don't think "Oh, I know it's just another of those fruity computers".

Pun rating:
Excellent. Almost as good as "Apple": "slice", "byte" – even "pie".

DiLL PiCKLE

Dill Pickle

More vegetably than other more fruity computers, ideal for those who really prefer their computers to sound a shade more vegetabley.

Pun rating:
Very good if the company get into trouble.

RADISH

Radish

An extremely vegetably sort of computer for those who like a touch of unabashed veggie.

Pun rating:
Zero.

Meeting other people

A new game for computer buffs. All you have to do is turn off your computer and try and conduct a normal relationship with other people.
Rating: a bit difficult, this one.

Shaving

All you have to do is turn off your computer, pick up a razor and shave off that ridiculous beard.
Rating: absolutely impossible.

Washing Under Your Arms

All you have to do is . . . come off it!
Rating: Nil.

Systems Variable Corner

One of the most useful systems variables on the Spectrum is known as FRAMES. Type in PRINT PEEK 23672, PEEK 23673 and it will tell you the latest snooker score.

QAZIQARGS OF QARGG!

A Role-play Fantasy Adventure Game For Bloody Big Kids

A PROGRAMME FOR YOU TO KEY IN TO YOUR SPECTRUM ONLY TO FIND THERE ARE TWO MISTAKES SOMEWHERE IN THE THREE THOUSAND AND ODD NUMBERS AND IT DOESN'T WORK UNLESS YOU SEND OFF FOR THE PRE-RECORDED TAPE IN FRUSTRATION.

In Alan Whizzkid's new sub-Tolkien game for rather sad people, you visit the Land Of Qargg to meet the Qaziqargs who have great powers of no imagination.

★ Can you get past the Magic Grxthyx?
★ Can you vanquish the Guardian of Nyrkkyr's Pool Of Pretentiousness?
★ Can you wield the Mystic Sword Of Absolute Garbage to obtain Jykyll's lost something else without any vowels in it?
★ Can you grow up?

JUST TYPE IN THE LISTING BELOW, DRESS UP IN A SILLY COSTUME AND AWAY YOU GO!

```
10 CLS:INPUT A$:PRINT "I'M SORRY,I DON'T
UNDERSTAND THAT":PAUSE 50:GOTO 10
```

PEOPLE WHO LOOK LIKE FISH.

Thinking about moving your business? Then think Peterborough. The business centre that's just far enough from London to be awkward and not quite near enough to the Midlands to be convenient. The business centre that's not really near a motorway but is extremely near to Wisbech. The business centre with a daily bus service to Kettering. And Corby. And a chance to see top fourth division football as well. Thinking about moving? Think Peterborough. Think not. For more information on the Peterborough effect:–

PETERBOROUGH: not as far away as you thought. Not as far away as you hoped. Peterborough Development Corporation, Peterborough, near nowhere.

Name_____

Position_____
(please enclose sketch)

_____

Tel._____

THE PETERBOROVGH EFFECT
IT'S BEEN WITH US FOR CENTURIES

BITZ

● **The Nolan Sisters In Concert** Yes they're coming to Wembley, as part of their sell-out world tour. Here's your chance to enter this great competition and win two *free!* **Nolan Sisters.**

Simply answer the following questions, then say in 15 words or less why you think the **Nolan Sisters** used to be on BBC 2 a lot. a) Because they always wear those tight satin trousers, how many of the girls suffer from chronic cystitis? b) Because of what urinary disorder do the girls always dance like their knees are strapped together? c) Which of the sisters quit the group to achieve oblivion in her own right? d) On the album NOLAN SISTERS GREATEST HITS, VOL 2, there is a song that was a hit (though not for them). Can you name it? e) Why is this book attacking the **Nolan Sisters**, when there are many other more deserving targets, like **Donald Sinden**, whom we haven't had a real go at for over five pages?

BEATLES ARE BACK TOGETHER!

ARE BEATLES BACK TOGETHER? Yes, They are! This time it's no media nonsense, because the *Fab Four*, minus **John**, are reforming sometime next year for a reunion concert. Although **Paul McCartney** will not be appearing, it's going to be Beatle Mania all over again! Just the thought of **George** and **Ringo** without **George** gigging again has record companies reaching for their cheque books. The Sixties will be swinging again – mini skirts, chelsea boots, bubble cars and **John F. Kennedy. Ringo,** who will not be appearing, said: "I wish them every success".

THE STYLE COUNCIL

Kids are good

Grown-ups are bad

Vote Labour, Vote Labour

Vote Labour, Vote Labour

Vote vote vote Labour.

---

julian lennon

Imagine I'm my father
It isn't hard to do
I sing exactly like him
And I look just like him too.
Imagine all my records
Selling by the ton
For the simple reason
I'm John Lennon's son.

© J. LENNON

SOUNDMASTER BIG BUCK

THE NEW YORK KING OF SCRATCH TALKS FRANKLY TO SMASH HITS

SH What are the origins of scratch mixing?
SBB W-w-w-w- weh! Wuh wuh weh! Wuh wuh well.. Scratch-atch-atch-atch . . . W-w-w-w- weh! Wuh, wuh, well, scratch sc-sc-sc-sc-sc-scratch well well scratch scratch cuh cuh cuh comes. Well scratch comes fuh fuh-fuh from.
Well, scratch atch comes from New York disco sub-culture sub.
Suh suh suh sub.
Culture.
Well.
(INSTRUMENTAL BREAK)
New scratch well new suh-suh-suh sub York ork well come.
come.
Come.
COME! COME! COME!
New yor-yor-yor.
SH Soundmaster Big Buck, thank you.
SBB Yuh-yuh you're wel. Well. Welcome. Come. Cuh . . .
SH Don't bother.

★ SUPERSTAR ★ ★ ★ ★

PROFILE

steve wright

RADIO ONE DJ THE ONE WITH THE GLASSES

"It's not as easy as people think, being a *DJ*. Some people think you just sit around and put records on. That's just not true – somebody else does that. No, there's a real skill, an art to being a *DJ*. It's not just a question of picking the records – somebody else does that. It's not even a question of thinking up rotten jokes – people send them in. What you've got to be good at is sitting down on chairs, and standing up on TOP OF THE POPS." He adopts his "MR. NOT-VERY-FUNNY OF PURLEY" voice. "TOP OF THE POPS is so crazy, you never know what mad thing's going to happen next. Sometimes, a balloon might float at your face, another time, it'll be a streamer, or Dave Lee Travis might wear a silly hat. And if you make a mistake, there's absolutely nothing you can do. Other than re-record it. You have to be young in this game, hardly any of the Radio One *DJ*'s fought in the Great War, except for Dave Lee Travis and Jimmy Savile. And I did, a bit. We've all got our completely different styles. For instance I wear glasses. Peter Powell doesn't. Janice Long wears things. And Steve Wright wears thin. I get recognised everywhere I go, of course, people say 'There's that *DJ* git. The one with the glasses'."

(STEVE WRIGHT IS CURRENTLY OPENING A NEW ASDA SUPERSTORE IN ESSEX. BY MISTAKE THIS INTERVIEW WAS CONDUCTED WITH PETER POWELL)

ALBUMS

MARILLION: Foxtrot Marillion are a completely different sound. New and original, the band defies pigeon-holing. Their unique blend of early GENESIS and late GENESIS, puts them at the forefront of modern rock bands who sound like GENESIS. According to the sleeve notes, Marillion's musical roots derive from "jazz, soul, funk, rock, blues and not GENESIS, no siree" Strange then that this album should start with "Watcher Of The Pies" which sounds remarkably like the famous GENESIS track "Watcher Of The Skies" with the letters "sk" replaced by "p" throughout. "This makes me really furious" said lead singer Fish in a recent TV interview. "It's like saying our concept track 'Supper's Nearly Ready' is like the GENESIS concept track 'Supper's Ready'. And it must be annoying for them, because it's plainly untrue. As for the album – I thought it was brilliant. There's only one comparison for a band this good is the Seventies super group, GENESIS."

MADONNA: Shag Happy The first thing that strikes one about the album is the naked picture of Madonna on the cover. Inside – an impressive variety of moods here, starting with the haunting "Ooh, Come On Babe, Screw Me Now", through the lilting ballad "Shaft me Sideways" to the up-tempo "Poke Me Through" and the tear-jerker "Stuff me Quickly". For me, the album is worth buying for the single alone, the cheeky and suggestive track "Drop your Pants, Sonny and give me a Good Long Hard Seeing-To with that Ramrod of Yours".

PRINCE FAXX

- Prince has never heard of Little Richard, Jimi Hendrix *or* Michael Jackson.

- Prince's real name is Mr. Prince.

- Prince's tongue is over six feet long.

- Prince has never taken drugs, nor has Mick Jagger.

- Prince is *not* a real prince!

- Prince has been growing a moustache for 10 years – but he's kept it a secret from his fans.

- Prince's favourite food is flies.

- Prince sleeps around.

- Prince failed his motorcycling proficiency test, because his feet couldn't reach the pedals.

- Prince's first film "Purple Rain" was not really any good.

- Despite his onstage image, in his private life, Prince is a pratt.

- Some of the above facts are not true!

BOB MUGELDORF

"Do They Know It's Hal-Al-Tel-Adjish?"

The crisis in Britain has shocked many of us in the Third World. Pictures on our television screens have brought home to us just how poorly off the British are: their economy's in ruins, their currency is worthless, and Bob Geldof cannot even afford a razor.

Please help them out by buying this record this Christmas.

FRANKIE GOES DOWNHILL
WELCOME TO
THE
SAME RECORD AS LAST TIME

"Lust in the Dionysian age is the Duty of the Existentialist Prophet talking of which, thar'll be £3.95, suckers!"

$[££ + $  $ + ⚽] + ∞ =$ **FRANKIE!**

Hype + Bullshit + Talentless Liverpudlians + Trevor Horn = Frankie

Frankie – Trevor Horn = Not much to be honest

ZBK
zum bang ching
thank you very much records

FRANKIE SAY ANYTHING PAUL MORLEY TELLS THEM TO SAY
T-Shirts (£17.50 + p&p)

13

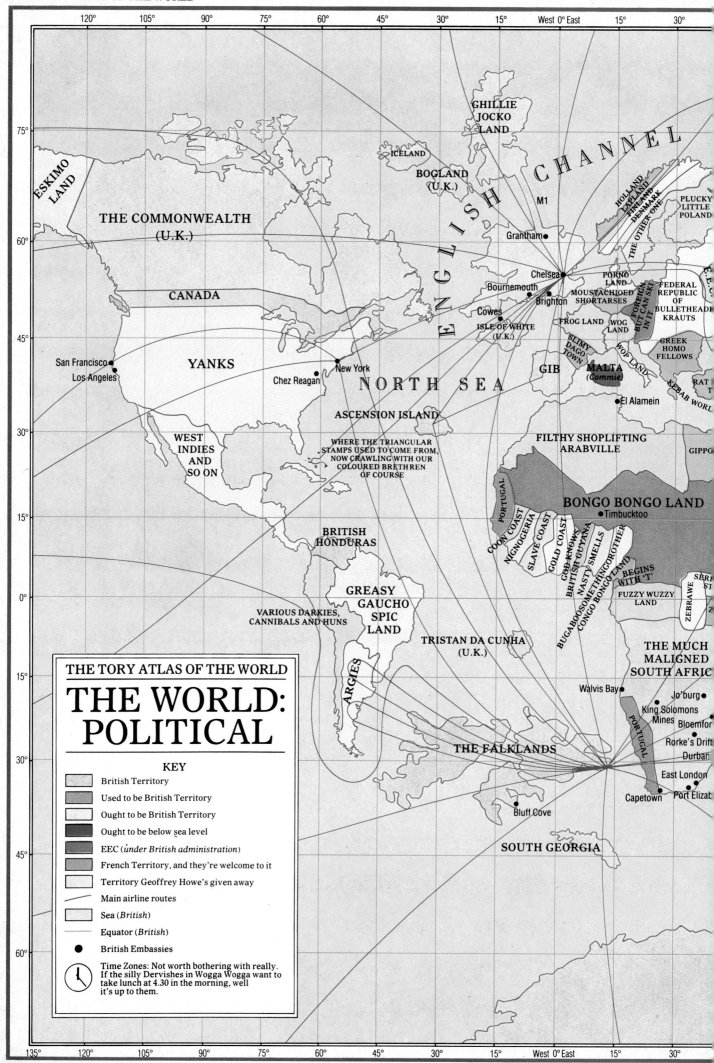

THE TORY ATLAS OF THE WORLD

THE WORLD: POLITICAL

KEY

British Territory

Used to be British Territory

Ought to be British Territory

Ought to be below sea level

EEC (*under British administration*)

French Territory, and they're welcome to it

Territory Geoffrey Howe's given away

Main airline routes

Sea (*British*)

Equator (*British*)

● British Embassies

Time Zones: Not worth bothering with really. If the silly Dervishes in Wogga Wogga want to take lunch at 4.30 in the morning, well it's up to them.

WEAKLY 80p

"Oh no! I've been washed up on a cartoon!"

INSIDE: Business, Computers, Travel, Property, Food, Wine, Accountancy. NEXT WEEK: Special "Humour" Issue.

ALAN

M

"Nuclear shelters are to include copies of the humourous magazine "Paunch" to help survivors cope with the stress of post holocaust life"

FT 1963

Alan Coren takes an amusing sideways look at what might happen if Dickens found himself in a nuclear shelter with only Paunch to read.

"Lawks a'mercy, Mrs Coren," said Dickens! "Don't you know a good pastiche when you see one"! "Cornish Pastiche," said Mrs Coren. "Not on your flippin' nellie." Old Boothroyd

"Do you think anyone's reading the article?"
"No, they're all looking at this cartoon . . ."

raised h
tureen a
duced a
er of lon
les. You
en stow
m neatly
magazin
ugh Lor
ws why.
me, 'ou
an", quo
greybear
ing his
with top
ferences
il knows
folkum
'oung, w
y right
hougthe
nowed a

W

Readers are invited to demonstrate that they are a lot funnier than Paunch writers.

Original 1897 caption: ELDERLY GENTLEMAN FINDING HIM
ILL FORTUNE IN THE PRESENCE OF THE NEW VICAR WITH A
LADY WHOSE CONSIDERABLE CHARMS HAVE CONTRIBUTED C
TO A STATE OF REASONABLE AGITATION IN THE AFOREMEN
OLDER CITIZEN REMARKING TO HIS LADY WIFE WHO H
NOTICED THE NEWFANGLED CLERICAL HABIT WHICH THE VIC
CHOSEN TO DRESS IN THAT IN OTHER CIRCUMSTANCES IT M
TRUE TO SAY THAT WHEREAS THE CLERGYMAN WAS INDEED
OF DISTINCTION THAT HE HIMSELF . . . (CONTINUED NEXT W

ROGER WADDALOADA
(After Andrew Marvell)
Had we but world enough and time
I would not work for the Radio Times.
I would sit down and think which way
To make contemporary doggerel pay.

Issue No. 1. £8.50

Cringing Royalist

THE HITCHHIKERS GUIDE TO THE GALAPAGOS

How Princess Elizabeth met the simple kebab-herd who became her Consort

IN COLOUR: THE QUEEN'S INTESTINES: How long are they really?

QUIZ: ARE YOU A MEMBER OF THE ROYAL FAMILY? Answer: No

PLUS! THE DAY THE QUEEN GOT OFFERED A BETTER JOB – Exclusive

SPOKESMEN ● EQUERRIES ● OGILVIES ● UNICORNS ● MUSH ● DENIALS ● WOGAN

The Intruder Press Published by gracious permission of Sir Donald Sinden

SECRET SEX LIFE OF THE ROYALS

The Royal Family strongly disapprove of using eye-catching headlines like the one above to attract the reader to an otherwise mind-bendingly tedious article. A Palace spokesman graciously informed us: ". . . if you expect any further co-operation out of us for your putrid little rag, kindly do not attempt to beef up the usual drivel by suddenly putting things like

LESBIAN TENDENCIES

In bold type without the slightest justification". So instead we shall burble on vaguely about the Queen being fond of animals. She is frequently to be seen, wrapped up snug in wellington boots and Brinksmat van, mucking out her herd of short-hair Millwall Casuals at Balmoral. Prince Philip told us; "That's a bloody lie and you know it you disgusting little tick, now get out of my Range Rover before I blow your balls off." Prince Philip is of course, in his own words, "a bloody foreigner", though this is a distinct advantage as the Royal Family are hardly ever in the country.

But thanks to his education – Mykonos Mixed Infants and Gordounstoun (where ▷

*T*he Queen, you may be interested to know, has a number of children. Four of them are largely her own work, but she is also Mother to 700 million "piccaninnies" around the Commonwealth. But she is just as fond of her own brood as she is of the people who dance naked around her offering boiled yak in the basket and shitting on her red carpets and so on.
   Though Prince Charles enjoys an active social life (right) he suffers from epistotumuliphobia – the fear that the post-box "won't work" on a really important letter. Unlike other Royals, he does not enjoy urinating in the sink when staying in hotels.
   Above: *Not just good friends!*
   Right Top: *St. Queen Mum of Glamis.*
   Right Centre: *Prince Edward (M.A. Cantab) is Chairman of Cambridge University's Keep Politics Out Of Genocide Society.*

he correctly answered the question "Did You Know That A Swan Can Break Your Arm With Its Wing?" well within the time allowed) – few nowadays would guess Prince Philip's ghastly secret were it not for the whiff of his "Hoummous de Faberge" Body Shampoo.

Whereas Viscount Linley hopes to become King by throwing bread rolls and cutting off people's ties, Prince William (above) has other ideas. Already a Brigadier-General in the Coldstream Guards he is currently attending an SAS Chaplain's Training Course.

BIG BLACK THROBBING LUMPS OF MEAT

This is the way the French think of horses, a view the Queen certainly does not share. She likes horses, but not with mint sauce. She is also an enthusiastic church-goer (*below*) and her favourite quotation from the bible is: "And God made the creeping things that crawl upon the earth and on the fourth day the French made them into soup."

(Genesis 1, 33)

Prince Charles: Has he gone bonkers?

NO

This is the first-ever exclusive picture of the legendary Duke and Duchess of Hampshire. Outwardly quite normal, they suffer from congenital deformities too horrible and titillating to describe here. Doctors believe these are caused by the insane 15th century practice of intermarriage between the Royal Family and the Spanish. Recipients of a £450,000 Grant from the Secret Vote of the Civil List, their duties include being walled up since birth in a 345-room potting-shed at Sandringham, and being the Official Winners of those Reader's Digest competitions that nobody believes in.

KICKER
A NEW NOVEL
BY WILLIAM GOLDMAN

CHAPTER ONE
This was gonna be the best goddam book he'd ever written.
Better than "Marathon Man".
Better than "Magic".
Better than "Control".
Better than "Tinsel".
The fucking-A-One-Absolute Best.
Forget "Butch Cassidy".
Forget "All the President's Men".
Forget "A Bridge Too Far"
FOR CRISE SAKES.
This was gonna be the ab-fu-so-uking-lutely BEST.

Two reasons:
1) He was William Goldman.
2) He was the master the goddam master of the kicker.

CHAPTER TWO
Nero licked the blood from his lips. That had been fun. But now he was angry. Angry the little girl had died so quickly. Nero was a sadist. But not an ordinary sadist. He worked at being a sadist. And now he was the best goddam sadist there ever was.
But he had a PROBLEM.
He wouldn't appear again until Chapter 4. So what the Hell was going on in the other chapters that he didn't know about??

CHAPTER THREE
Jackie hated her sister.
That was the main thing you had to know about Jackie.
Oh, and she was pretty.
But not just pretty. PRETTY!
She was only the most beautiful goddam woman in the goddam Universe. That's all. All in all, she was perfect. Except.
Except she was dead.

CHAPTER FOUR
William Goldman breathed a sigh of relief as he came back into the story. He was in CONTROL. He could make the strands come together. No-one else could. He was the master of the strands.

THE MASTER OF THE STRANDS
Jackie was his brother who'd had a sex change. And Nero, Nero, the sadist, was only four years old. And he'd eaten his sister. Only, get this: Nero was a dog. A FREAKIN' DOG!!
And Goldman was working for the CIA. The writing was a cover. And that was it.
That was the end of the novel. Except it WASN'T a novel. It was a letter. A LETTER! A letter Goldman was writing to HIMSELF. Only here's the kicker: Goldman. Was. A. Computer. And this wasn't the end of the novel. It was the start.

THE END

BE BRAVE LITTLE NODDY!

BE BRAVE LITTLE NODDY!

"Oh Big Ears" said Noddy "I don't think I will ever be happy ever again!"
"Of course you will" said Big ears, "Now let's make up a Brave Song – you're good at making up songs – think of a really nice Brave Song that will cheer yourself up!"
"I can't" said Noddy his head nodding sadly.
"Oh what does it matter if things go wrong, I'll sing and I'll whistle . . . dear dear I'm not very good at making up songs" sighed Big Ears. "I know how that ought to go!" said Noddy cheering up. "Like this Big Ears just you listen!" and he nodded his head as he began to sing,

"Oh, what does it matter
If things go wrong
I'll sing and I'll whistle
The whole day long
Oh what does it matter
If skies are grey
I'll sing and be happy
and jolly and gay
Oh what does it matter
If things aren't so merry
And death shrouded corpses
Lie ready to bury
Oh what does it matter
The angst ridden torment
The burning hot stench of
flesh cast asunder

Cold angry terror of
skull torn body
Gut wrenching fear
in stinking hollow
The blood red taste
of gas upon us
Dull thud of mortar in
clinging mud hole
The blind don't see
the soldier boy
Cry lifeless pain
on twisted wire
And all around the
taste of death
A slowly rotting
silent death

Noddy sang this very loudly in his little high voice and danced all around Big Ears as he sang, nodding his head till his bell jingled quite madly.
"I don't know what you're so bloody happy about" said Big Ears when Noddy at last stopped "You've just spoilt my whole bloody evening!"

THE FABER GOLDEN TREASURY OF TASTELESS AUTOGRAPH BOOK JOKES WRITTEN BY DESPERATE UNEMPLOYED KIDS Ed. Pete Townshend. £4.95

JENNINGS AND THE HORMONE IMPLANTS

When Jennings decides to enter the school cross country race he elects to use a little extra help in his preparations and persuades Derbyshire to lend a hand with a course of hormone implants.

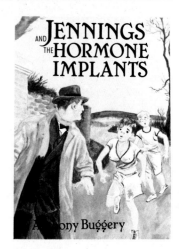

"What have you two boys been up to?" scoffed Mr Carter angrily as the two boys stumbled the last few yards into the school grounds, Jennings heaving breasts straining to be free of his flimsy cotton vest.
"Nothing Sir" replied Jennings his tender young bosom thrust upwards in an aggrandibular display of sexual bravado.
So starts another Jennings talk, and as ever the two young chums are up to their necks in trouble. But when Jennings discovers a new use for his firm young breasts in the school boiler house things start to look up.
"I'll be glad to get out of this brassiere and into something a little more relaxing" chortles Jennings as Mr Wilkinson explains the Latin prep to the boys trying hard not to admire Jennings magnificent young cleavage.

Now read on . . .

By the same author:
- JENNINGS HAS TWEAKY NIPPLES
- JENNINGS BUYS A NEW DRESS
- JENNINGS GRADUALLY BEGINS TO FEEL MORE AT EASE WHEN HE IS WITH OTHER WOMEN
- JENNINGS SPENDS AN INTIMATE EVENING WITH A SIGNALS OFFICER FROM THE ROYAL NAVY ORDNANCE CORPS
- JENNINGS UNDERGOES SPECIALIST SURGERY
- MRS JENNINGS HAS TWINS

THE FABER BOOK OF JINGLES ed. Simon Brett £11.95
Collected in Suffolk 14th June 1902
From the singing of the Cooper Family at Lowestoft

The Trawling Trade

VERSE: COME GATH-ER ROUND, YOU SAIL-ORS AND LISTEN TO MY SONG IT'S OF A CRU-EL CAP-TAIN IN A WRAP AROUND SA-RONG. I'VE SAILED THE SEVEN SEAS, MY LADS, ALL ON THE RA-GING MAIN, BUT I'M NOT VERY KEEN ON FISH FINGERS 'COS I KNOW WHAT THEY'RE MADE OF

CHORUS: GOE DOWN CAPTAIN BIRD'S EYE! GOE DOWN, GOE DOWN! TALKIN' BOUT YOUR BROCCOLI SPEARS AND YOUR SUPER MOUSSE AND YOUR ARCTIC-ROLL. GOE DOWN CAPTAIN BIRD'S EYE! GOE DOWN. GOE DOWN! WITH YOUR CRISPY COD ı FRIES AND YOUR PETIT POIS AND YOUR FAGGOTS ALL IN RICH GRA-VY - OH.

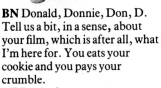

BARRY NORMAN

DONALD SINDEN

BARRY NORMAN catches DONALD SINDEN on the set of his latest film, "*Danger At Work*"

Donald Sinden explains how famous he is to the tea lady on the set of his latest blockbuster movie.

BN Donald, Donnie, Don, D. Tell us a bit, in a sense, about your film, which is after all, what I'm here for. You eats your cookie and you pays your crumble.

DS Pardon?

BN What's this film all about?

DS It's a tragedy, in which I play a rather sad character, who has difficulties adjusting to every day life. He's not terribly good at his job, and in a way, that's what the film's about. The plots terribly Pinteresque. It's about a man who gets his hair caught in an unguarded machine and suffers an appalling industrial accident.

BN Oh, it's an industrial training film?

DS Well . . . that's only part of it really. There is another wonderful sequence, in which the character I play works at a machine that *is* guarded, and comes to no harm at all. I think what the film's trying to say is that, in a very real way, it's safer to use a machine which is guarded, rather than one which,

say, isn't. A lot of films these days don't have a message. Whereas ours has one printed at the end in big letters. I think that's terribly important, don't you?

BN "Don't leave your machine unguarded."

DS That's *my* line, you swine. My agent took months getting me this part . . .

BN Which in a way is where we end the interview.

Donald Sinden is a member of the Royal Shakespeare Book Club

"*DANGER AT WORK*" (running time 7½ minutes) opens at the Granada Assembly plant, Dagenham on July 4.

SPECIAL FX NEWS

THIS WEEK THOSE HORRIFIC SANDWORMS FROM "DUNE"

Many people were amazed when they saw Dino Di Laurentis' giant worms on the screen for the first time. Just how did he make them look like enormous pieces of cardboard wiggling around on the end of a coat hanger?

Head of the 300 man "Dune" worm effects team, Jim Incompetent explains:

"Well, we had this vast budget, and we employed all the latest technology to spend it. Cash points, VISA, American Express, computer modem withdrawals, traveller's cheques and Eurobonds."

WHAT DID HE SPEND IT ON.
"Cardboard mostly. But, obviously in a movie like this, you can't just get by on cardboard, and we were pretty lavish with glue, cling-film and even squeezy bottles."

WHAT WAS THE BIGGEST PROBLEM?
"Realism. We wanted to make the worms look and move in a believable way. It was incredibly difficult."

SO HOW DID YOU SOLVE IT
"We didn't."

Sandworm . . . as you saw it on the screen

ON THE GRAPEVINE

One of Hollywood's top liars re-writes a whole load of PR handouts sent to her by agents and makes up the rest . . .

* * * * * * * * * * * *

Richard Burton and Elizabeth Taylor are to get back together again, now that Burton hasn't touched a drop for over a year.

* * * * * * * * * * * *

DONNY OSMOND, ex of the Jackson Five, was attacked in Salt Lake City by a group of chickens. They stole his wallet and all his credit cards. Donny had to walk home one hundred miles completely naked to get help.

* * * * * * * * * * * *

STAR SECRET Dolly Parton wears a toupee. On her breasts!

* * * * * * * * * * * *

Poor old one armed Steven Spielberg has fallen hopelessly in love with Dustin Hoffman, recently recovered from Legionnaire's Disease. The two were seen recently having it off in a smart Los Angeles restaurant.

* * * * * * * * * * * *

Robert De Niro is Al Pacino

Frank Sinatra is not a member of the Mafia! And that's official!!

Jenny Agutter has got three buttocks — and none of them work.

* * * * * * * * * * * *

ABC FILM GUIDE

SEQUEL III (PG)
How could there only be two? The third in the smash hit 'Sequel' series Probably starring Harrison Ford

'SEVERAL SPOTTY ADOLESCENTS ATTEMPT TO LOSE THEIR VIRGINITY IN A NUMBER OF UNLIKELY WAYS – 2' (X)
Featuring nobody you've ever heard of, or will ever hear of again.

Woody Allen's **'GOODBYE SENSE OF HUMOUR'** (PG)
An extremely serious film Starring Woody Allen & Woody Allen's Girlfriend

a DAVID LEAN film

'Worthy' PG

Adapted from a dull novel that nobody ever thought of doing before

SCREENPLAY BY **DAVID LEAN**   DIRECTED BY **DAVID LEAN**

A **DAVID LEAN** PRODUCTION

Featuring the Indian People, except for the main role which is played by a white man blacked up in the most interesting way

THIS IS A DAVID LEAN POSTER

Mel Brooks IN A MEL BROOKS MOVIE

TOTALLY OBSESSED by *Nazis* PG

SCREENPLAY BY **MEL BROOKS & ADOLF HITLER**

From an original joke by **MEL BROOKS**

As featured in the book "I'M NOT TOTALLY OBSESSED BY NAZIS, MEIN FUHRER"

No 8396   Price 50p (inc. compu business news)

THE SUNDAY TIMES

14 APRIL 1985

10 Rillington Place

Sun Times Discreet Upmarket Finance Game

Legseleven	11	Unluckyforsome	13
Twofatladies	88	Verylargethatsize	58
Fattadyandleg	81	Unluckyfatswan	1382
Onitsown	1	Tiddlydumdum	91
Thirtynine ladies	39	Tiddlydeedee	93
Legstwelve	12	Key to the horse	69
Swanandfatlady	28	Fourfatisotopes	56
Luckyforswans	47	Nothinparticular	62
Legsonabadger	4	Sixtysacrowd	60
Mothermakesfive	5	Horseylatlady	48

LAST WEEKS £20,000 "NOTBINGO" WINNER
Dr. Sir Bernard Professor CBE, FRICS.

LEAD IN PENCILS SHOCK

p 13

DIANA'S ILLEGITIMATE BLACK BABY

p 22 (but not this week)

IN COLOUR

Are black stoc really sexy? A pictorial

SALT TALKS THREAT

US to deploy 120 new medium-range Union Carbide factories

p 14

MONKEY SCROTUM FACELIFTS

p 19

Royal Nazi star Shi'ite leak

THERE WAS confusion in the Pentagon today over President Reagan's detailed proposals for the strategic interstellar weapons programme (STINTWEP). In a heated memorandum to NASA from inside the Pentagon it has become apparent that whilst the chiefs of the armed services are happy with the Laser missile guidance capacity and the ICBM Knockout facilities, they are concerned at the role of what the President refers to as 'The Wookie'. This wookie, according to a highly placed source in the state department, has no clear function in the programme although in conjunction with the mysterious 'Han Solo' he appears to be at the centre of the President's long-term strategy. This strategy has been de-

length with the President defining his priorities as follows:
a) The investment in systems which can eliminate Russian Intercontinental missiles as they leave the earth's atmosphere.
b) To provide umbrella protection for US strategic and defensive missile systems in their silos.
c) To rescue Princess Leia from the evil Darth Vader and thereby the Deathstar.

Military experts admit to being puzzled by the latest point and also by the President's additional wish that a Mr Luke Skywalker be given overall control of the project.

When questioned on the Whitehouse Lawn in his weekly briefing, the President appeared confused and asleep. On being woken by close

By Simon Drumpanty in Washington; Aenone Stools and Hunter Clung in Calcutta; Gloag McNaughtie, Siobiofarouagh O'Rioauroiagh and Ken Nervous in Belfast; Imam Bayildi & Sarah-Felicity Minge in Beirut; Morrison G Potato III in Los Angeles; Bute Freeloader and Rory Wastrel in Brenda Cavity in the Zanzibar; Organa Prule & Nimoy Dungeonquest in Addis Ababa; Kathy Smartass aboard Soyuz 33 and Christnose Ouse-Manning in the office in London.

Nancy?' He then refused to answer detailed questions on the controversial scheme saying only, 'God bless America – May The Force Be With

At Heathrow last night, Mrs Thatcher expressed her 'concern and anguish over this tragic outrage' though privately she is known to have said sorry what was the question again. Looking blood-boltered and fur-stained despite her seal culling Winter Break in the Falklands, she refused to comment on the latest Government leak, preferring to chunter on for hours about drugs, bicycles and football. MPs on both sides of the fence this week proclaimed themselves both alarmed and disgusted at the leak of what is claimed to be the Official Leaving Card for Mr Neil Kinnock. Despite Mr Kinnock's insistence that he has never heard of it, the card appears to be genuine and several years old. Parliamentary staff were today still

circumstances surrounding the leak, but it would appear that someone may have been able to gain access to the notice-board where embarrassing documents are kept.

In the early hours of this morning, police swooped on the house in North London where all the murderers live, smashing drug rings and furniture and arresting hooligans. Noel Edmonds was travelling at over 32 mph in his beautiful girlfriend and enormous Italian car when stopped.

Hence our exclusive repetition that Princess Michael of Kent's father *was* a Nazi. But Von Reibnitz served in fact only briefly in the Herrlichengruppe (or 'Nice') SS, sometimes known as Hitler's Redcoats. He himself only joined the Nazi party for the riding

to become one of the small number of 'Horsemensch von der Apocalypse'. His sole function was to sell value-for-money Kia-ora and busk to the infamous death-queues. In any case, whatever the past, it is clearly not Princess Michael

of Ke s faul hat s is a me ber of e Roy Family everal

Good riddance, you Welsh windsock.
I knew you'd never last.
Denis Healey
Not as easy as you thought, was it smartass. M. Foot.
"It has not been an enjoyable experience staring all day across the dispatch at someone whose nose has a foreskin. Yours sincerely Margaret Thatcher

House debates common potato policy

by Our Photocopying Staff

Hansard – September 17th 1985 p.m.

Mr Michael Meacher (*Lab., Oldham W*) Wurghh! Wurghh! Wurghh! Wurg! Wurrrghh! Wug!

Mr Norman Tebbit (*C., Chingford*) Phwar! Phwar! Phwarr! Wurrrghh! Phwarrr! Wurrrgh!

Sir Anthony Beaumont-Dark (*C., Birmingham, Selly Oak*) Gnarri! Gnarri! Gargi! Garl! Garra! Glarg! Glarr! Wurghh! Phwarr! Glarrghh! Arglgargh! Klargllllllgggghh!

Mr Gerald Kaufman (*Lab., Manchester, Gorton*) Yurgh! Yurgh! Yurgh! Wurgh! Phwarr! Yurgh!

Mr Michael Heseltine (*C., Henley*) Naiirr! Naiirr! Nanairrr!

Dr David Owen (*SDP All., Plymouth, Devonport*) Nairr! Phwarr! Wurrrg! Hough! Hough! Phwarr! Wurgh! Wurg! Cacacacacaca!

Sir Geoffrey Howe (*C., Surrey E.*) Hough!

Mr Dennis Skinner (*Lab., Bolsover*) Peet! Peet! Weem! Klarirrrrrgggh! Yargayar-gayargayargayarga! Agoooo! Quag Quag quag quag! Agoooooooo! Agooo! Skwarri! Schiurgsgggg! A g g a ! A g g a a a a ! Schurrrgggghh! Agga agga agga agga agga agga! Phwarr! Wurgh! Ca ca ca ca ca ca! Hough! Argargargargargarg-argargargargaaarrgh!

Should we arm the football hooligans?

THIS MAY now be the only option left if we are ever to get Peregrine Worsthorne to atomise himself in an apoplectic explosion. Previous attempts to achieve his removal from the planet – poisoned venison, defenestration, beg-

---

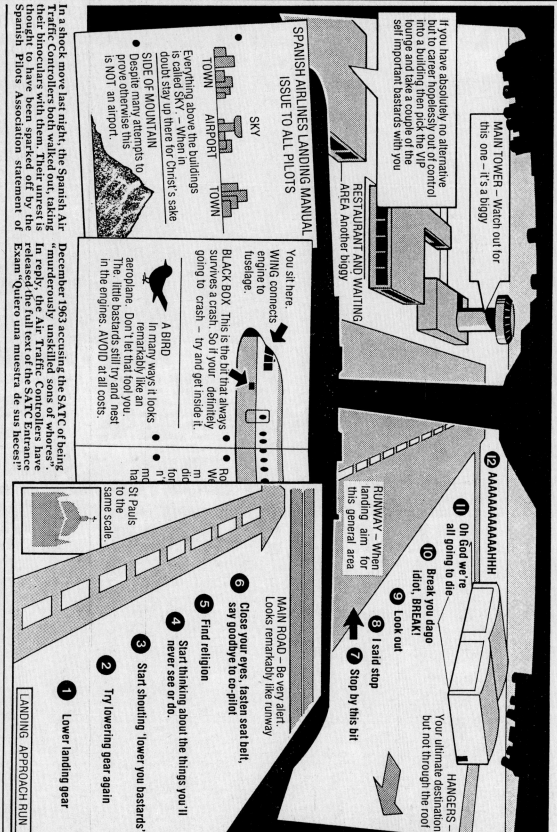

Spanish air traffic control

Phill E. Stine

MAIN TOWER – Watch out for this one – it's a biggy

RESTAURANT AND WAITING AREA Another biggy

**SPANISH AIRLINES LANDING MANUAL
ISSUE TO ALL PILOTS**

SKY

TOWN   AIRPORT   TOWN

SIDE OF MOUNTAIN

- Everything above the buildings is called SKY. – When in doubt stay up there for Christ's sake

- Despite many attempts to prove otherwise this is NOT an airport.

You sit here. WING connects engine to fuselage.

BLACK BOX This is the bit that always survives a crash. So if your definitely going to crash – try and get inside it.

A BIRD In many ways it looks remarkably like an aeroplane. Don't let that fool you. The little bastards still try and nest in the engines. AVOID at all costs.

- Ro...
  We...

- m...
  di...
  for...
  n'...
  ma...
  ha...

St Pauls to the same scale.

⑫ AAAAAAAAAAAHHH

⑪ Oh God we're all going to die

⑩ Break you dago idiot, BREAK!

⑨ Look out

⑧ I said stop

HANGERS – Your ultimate destination but not through the roof

RUNWAY – When landing aim for this general area

MAIN ROAD – Be very alert. Looks remarkably like runway

⑦ Stop by this bit

⑥ Close your eyes, fasten seat belt, say goodbye to co-pilot

⑤ Find religion

④ Start thinking about the things you'll never see or do.

③ Start shouting 'lower you bastards'

② Try lowering gear again

① Lower landing gear

LANDING APPROACH RUN

In a shock move last night, the Spanish Air Traffic Controllers both walked out, taking their binoculars with them. Their unrest is thought to have been sparked off by the Spanish Pilots Association statement of

December 1963 accusing the SATC of being "murderously unskilled sons of whores". In reply, the Air Traffic Controllers have released the full text of the SATC Entrance Exam "Quiero una muestra de sus heces?"

WINKIE SHRINKAGE

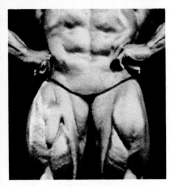

Champion body-builder, Hunk Lummocks writes . . .

Sooner or later every body-builder faces the terrible dilemma of winkie-shrinkage. As the rest of your body grows and develops, tragically, your little German Soldier remains the same size. No matter how proud and noble your frankfurter is initially, it inevitably winds up looking like one of the chipolatas in Heinz Sausage and Beans.

Simple remedy

There is no remedy, simple or otherwise, but just think of all the things you have, that normal men don't, like:
1 a hundred and eighty-inch neck
2 a vast and ugly network of veins the size of mooring rope over your entire body
3 strange muscles on the top of your shoulder blades
4 the ability not to be able to fit inside a mini.
See? Things aren't so bad, huh?

VIDEO CORNER

MUSCLE RATINGS:

ᘉᘉᘉᘉ *Masterpiece*

ᘉᘉᘉ *Brilliant but flawed*

ᘉᘉ *Poor*

ᘉ *Hardly any muscles at all*

CITIZEN KANE ᘉ
(b/w. dir. Orson Welles. USA 1936)
The film which catapulted Orson Welles to fame is now out on video. And it's a real turkey. Welles is fine as Kane, but I would have liked to see him pumping more iron. Not a posing pouch in sight as Kane rises to power as newspaper magnate who is singularly disinterested in body building. Where the film falls down is its inability to tackle head on the central issue of muscle-shaping. Instead it drones on about a sledge called 'Rosebud'. How just a couple of adjustable squat stands could have relieved the boredom here. Irritatingly, Welles makes the film, with its richly interwoven themes, far too complicated to watch doing any exercise more complicated than a simple flat-bench dip. Weedy.

PUMPING IRON ᘉᘉᘉ
(dir ? 197? Arnold Schwarzenegger)
This movie has *everything*: bench presses, dip curls, sissy squats, and excellent cinematography. ORSON – *TAKE NOTE.*

● NEW ● NEW ● NEW ● NEW ● NEW ● NEW ● NEW ● NEW ● NEW ●

Anabolic Steroid POISON CAPSULES

from
NATURE GOOD

★ *AS USED BY TOP EAST GERMAN HERMAPHRODITES*

You will actually see your body cells mutate. Hitherto only used in Nazi experiments – Now available from Naturegood Products.

● **Builds** up body fat
● **Clogs** up veins
● **Increases** heart-rate
● **Promotes** blindness and impotence.

GUINEA PIG OFFER:
Please rush me a month's supply of these evil tablets. If I'm not fully dead within six months you will rush me my money back.

Name (Print) ....

Address ....

....

Ex-world champion, KIRK TITE-BUTTOX writes: "I've been using this product for as long as I can remember – and I can remember everything! I can't recommend them more highly. Nnnnnaaaaaaaaaaaarrrr!"

Kirk Tite-Buttox

FULLY UNTESTED

● NEW ● NEW ● NEW ● NEW ● NEW ● NEW ● NEW ● NEW ● NEW ●

POSING A PROBLEM

It's probably the most important decision you'll ever make. Because once you've picked your posing pouch, it's with you for life.
Once your thigh muscles treble in size, these skimpy little briefs just won't come down.
No matter how hard you, or any of your friends pull. There's no getting them over those gargantuan quadriceps.
So you'll want to make sure, they look good, feel good and are flame-proof.

ZIPPO POSERS

Don't pick a pouch that makes you go 'ouch'

THE LITERARY ALLUSION THAT MADE A MAN OUT OF "ROCK"

30% BRAINIER IN ONE MONTH!
or your money back

Please rush me my CHARLES EINSTEIN © BRAINWORKER ™ *course*

My wrist measurement is over 21"

Name ....
Address ....
City .... State...................
Zone .... Zip Size.............

NEO-NARCIES MALEBAG

Dispute
Dear NN

Could you settle an argument. My body building partner says that World War II came *before* World War I. *I* say there only was one World War: number 2. Please prove me right, and lay to rest once and for all the myth that body-builders are stupid.

Sincerely
Dirk Squat

Myth
Dear NN

I was writing this letter to you, but now I've forgotten what I was going to say. I hope this lays to rest, once and for all, the myth that body-builders are stupid.

Sincerely
Rock Rock

Muscle
Dear NN

I have been body-building now for over thirty years, and have achieved the 300% build potential in every single muscle in my body. But people still laugh at me. Is it because I wear glasses?

Sincerely
The Michelin Man

100kg
Dear NN

I have been concentrating on my sphincter muscles, and now I can lift a 100kg weight with my ass.

Sincerely
Richard Head

Body
Dear NN

Once and for all – I'd like to lay body builders. That's a myth.

Sincerely
Vitamin K Johnson

BRAIN STRE-E-E-ETCHERS
Your brain's a muscle too! Work out on this.

a MAZE -ing

Help Jeff find his way to the jaccuzzi, where his training partner Dirk has removed his posing pouch.

National Blood Transfusion Service

GIVE EXCUSES

. . . not blood

I share a flat with three other men

I borrowed someone else's razor at college

I once lent my sleeping bag to a man in the Christian Union

I accidentally touched another man's bottom at the swimming baths the other day

I am a male nurse

I don't like the biscuits they give you afterwards

MR. T

One of acting's true heavyweights talks exclusively to NN

NN: How did you create the character of BA BARACCUSS?
Mr. T: *Who?*
NN: The guy you play in the "A" Team
Mr. T: *Well, I started on small weights, worked up to 150 kg on each arm. Then the neck. The neck's one of the most important parts of the character. So it was a program of bench presses, squat thrusts until I felt I'd got it right.*
NN: Do you think the character's developing at all?
Mr. T: *Sure. His pectorals are coming along nicely, and the triceps are improving all the time.*
NN: Is it really true you were once a six stone weakling?
Mr. T: *Yeah. But then I put on all this jewellery.*
NN: After playing an aggressive heavy black man in "ROCKY II" and a heavy, black aggressive man in "THE 'A' TEAM", do you feel you're in any way typecast?
Mr. T: *No. I've been offered a film as a black heavy aggressive man, then a part in a new TV show where I play a man who's black, aggressive and heavy. Then I'm going to play Liubov Andreevna in Checkov's "The Cherry Orchard".*
NN: Well, that's very different.
Mr. T: *It will be. I'm playing it with a machine gun. We're gonna blow up that mother of a cherry orchard.*
NN: Thank you, Mr. T. You can put me down now.

EXERCISE of the month

No. 181: The Butt-pat

This is a handy one you can do quickly in the showers *after* your work-out. The trick is to make it look casual, but to get enough power in the wrist to make the recipient squeal with delight. Try saying: 'Hey – nice curls you were doing out there, Jeff', or 'See ya Thursday, pal', or even 'Watch out – fly! . . . Got it!'

1 Open hand. Keep flat. (N.B.: *Make sure middle finger is not protruding*!!)

2 Flick forward, withdrawing sharply on impact.

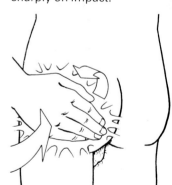

3 Laugh with masculine ferocity.

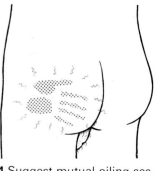

4 Suggest mutual oiling session.

NEO NARCISSISM

June 1927   Vol. 1 No. 1

incorporating Thick and Muscly Weekly

EXERCISE OF THE MONTH
The Pillow Bite

CHANGING ROOM ETIQUETTE
To dangle or not to dangle?

TUMOURS CAN LOOK GOOD!
They grow quick, too!

NIPPLE REMOVAL
Is it necessary?

PLUS! ALL OUR REGULAR FEATURES; NEWS, VIEWS, SCROTUM HANDCUFFS.

A LIFE DEDICATED TO BODY BUILDING

Is it perhaps a tiny, teensy-weensy, little bit futile? We find out why not.

THINGS I WISH I KNEW
NIGEL LAWSON

I wish I knew why I am Chancellor of the Exchequer. It's always puzzled me that one. I wish I knew what a Chancellor was supposed to do.

Also, I wish I knew why my name is an anagram of "WE ALL SIGN ON." What does it mean?

And also "LEANING OWLS," "ALL NINE WOGS" and "NIGS LEAN LOW."

But the one that terrifies me the most is "E. WANS NOLLIG." I hate that one. How would you feel if you knew that your name was an anagram of "E. WANS NOLLIG."

I wish I knew why, once a year, I have to go for an early morning walk with my family. And I wish I knew why the whole of Fleet Street comes along. And why this annual sortie gets on to the news. I've seen some pretty unsinteresting news items in my time – but a portly middle-aged man and his family throwing bread at some ducks takes the biscuit. Or was it biscuits we threw, and it takes the bread? I wish I knew. I wish I knew why I am writing this article.

I wish I knew when to stop. When people are bored. Er.

~~CHOLERA~~
~~T.B.~~
~~POLIO~~
~~SMALLPOX~~
PAUL DANIELS

PAUL DANIELS ERADICATION FUND
PLEASE GIVE GENEROUSLY

TOGETHER WE CAN BEAT PAUL DANIELS

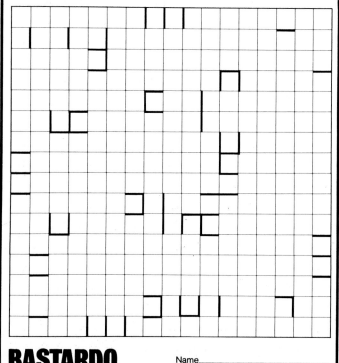

BASTARDO

No. 846. This week's Bastardo has no numbered squares – to make it more difficult.

Name_____

Address_____

_____

ACROSS
1 Pear fizz run out. Haven for Parasites (8)
2 Fullers adept at swapping Latin for English (16)
3 Front part of odd morals not repeating opening . . . oh forget it (1-4,6)
4 Far too difficult (3,3,9)
5 Impossible (10)
6 Ditto (5)
7 You'll never get it (5,5,3,2)
8 Sorry (5)
9 No chance (2,6)
10 Wish there was an anagram (4,5,3,2,7)
11 I'll try the Down clues (3,3,3,4,5)

DOWN
6 Looks as before – salami after (7)
9 Oh Christ (2,6)
14 He's just as bad (3,4,2,3)
17 I know (1,4)
26 I'll do the Brainteaser instead (3,2,3,11,7)
29 4 legged beast that barks (3)
30 Odd deb – place to sleep (3)
43 Ha, Ha (2,2)
51 That'll teach you to give up half way (2,5)
52 Simple (6)
53 Perserverance, that's all (12,5,3)

BRIDGE
Luke Coolhand

North and South, Mrs. Wood-Brown and Mrs Jones-Templeton face East and West, Mr Wood-Brown and Mr Jones-Templeton at the Jones-Templeton's last Friday evening:

♠ KJ86
♡ J93
◇ 32
♣ QJ92

♠ Q963　　　♠ 102
♡ K107652　♡ Q8
◇ KQ　　　　◇ 10974
♣ 3　　　　　♣ A10874

♠ A74
♡ A4
◇ AJ865
♣ K65

Bidding:

South	West	North	East
—	—	No	No
INT	2♡	dble (1)	redble
3◇	No	3NT	dble (2)
No	No	No	No
No	No	No	No

IN NEXT WEEK'S COLOUR MAGAZINE

LOTS OF ARTICLES THAT SOUND MUCH MORE INTERESTING THAN THE ONES YOU'VE BEEN READING IN THIS ISSUE BUT WHICH IN FACT TURN OUT TO BE JUST AS DULL AND BORING AS EVER

Excerpted from
GOSH THE THEATRE'S SUCH FUN, LOVE

The 15th Volume of Donald Sinden's Autobiography.
(*continued from page 121*)

and I'll never forget the thousands of dear, dear friends I've been privileged to make in the wonderful world of the theatre. Perhaps my favourite memory is of a party after the opening night of "Mother Goose" at the Eastbourne Palladium – a super, super play in which I played my first Hamlet. I was talking to Dame Peggy,[1] and suddenly up came Johnny Gielgud[2] and behind him were the Mills[3]. And you know what I said? No? Nor do I.

Chapter 20
Another terribly amusing incident was the first time I met Her Gracious Majesty, Her Royal Highness the Queen. I was hanging around Buckingham Palace in the hope of getting a K, and Her Majesty displayed her lovely sense of humour, when I emerged from inside a cupboard in her bedroom, and fell prostrate at her feet saying, "Go on! Please give me a knighthood!" You know what she said? I'll never forget it: "Guards! Arrest this dreadful old Ham!" What a hoot!

Chapter 27
Another time I met Her Gracious Sovereign whose loyal subject I am and always will be Ma'am, should you be reading one of the 20,000 copies I sent to the palace, was when I'd been playing the part of Widow Twankey in the lovely, lovely, famed 1942 stage production of "Carry On Up The Beanstalk!" She displayed her wonderful,

wonderful sense of humour when she said, "You were dreadful. Why don't you pack it in?" My, how we laughed!

Chapter 38
I'll never forget the first time I met Larry, a dear, dear friend, a close colleague, a man I was privileged to share a stage with, a warm human being and . . . who am I talking about? Oh yes, Noel Coward, and he displayed that gorgeous sense of humour when, at a party at his home after the opening night of a film I starred in[4], he said to me, "Who are you? You're not invited! Get out!" I always have this problem that I am so immersed in my roles that no one ever recognises me. It's called "Method Acting".

Chapter 41
On another occasion, Her Majesty asked for my autograph. Not directly, of course, but courtesy of Her Inspector of Taxes, a lovely, lovely man called Mr Wainwright, who wrote to me when I was playing Badger in (not continued)

Errata
p.438 Lord Olivier would like to make it clear that he is not and never has been, a "dear dear friend" of this Mr Sinden

p. 532 Mr Sinden inadvertently refers to himself as "Sir" Donald Sinden.

Footnotes
[1] "Dame Peggy" – not *the* Dame Peggy, but a very lovely bloke called Brian who was playing the Dame.
[2] That was what we all called him, although he was actually a lighting man called Sid.
[3] A reference to a pair of windmills used as scenery in the 1937 production of "Mother Goose".
[4] "Baby's First Xmas" (1960, Super 8. Dir. Mrs Sinden)

DRIBBLING PORKY LOINS

WHEN YOU THINK OF GREECE, YOU THINK OF TWO THINGS – BRILLIANT OPERA AND GREAT FOOD. BUBBELOS HAS BEEN THE MASTER CHEF AT THE AXILLA MEAT GRIDDLE IN PECKHAM FOR FIVE YEARS. HE TALKS ABOUT HIS LIFE, HIS ART, AND THE TIME HE GOT CAUGHT BY THE SANITATION INSPECTORS.

Allo mates, how you doin. People ask me: "Bubbie, how is kebab shop different of other restuarants?" And I say: "In kebab shop you bring the dustbins *in*!" In Greece, where from I come, there is very long tradition of "Take-away" kebabs. Many hundred of years ago, a rich man he would say; "Hey. I have a kebab which is stinking out my kitchen, would you take it away?" And some boy would say "yes", and he take it away. They certainly wouldnt pay for it no chance matey, and never would ever they eat it. But here is England everything is upside-out crazy, and the kebab she is regarded as food. Crazy, innit? In my country, the kebab she is what lepers wear round their necks, so that even deaf people know they are coming. The alarm would be raised double quick time, sure. "Hey can you smell that? – there is a bloody leper on the other side of the mountain."

Now listen, I tell you a other funny things. Many peoples they dont realise the Donner Kebab she is actually a nanimal in fact. When they see the cylyndrical slob of greasy oozing brown meat rototating in my shop, they think "Hey-what kind of nanimal is supposed to look like that fellow? Is probably bits of rabbitses eyelids and cow's sphinctres compressed and reformed and that." Wrong. The donner kebab she is in fact actually the world's only completely boneless animal, and frolicks freely in her natural home in the foothills of Panos, you know. The donner she is also the sweatiest creature in the Animal Kingdom (the sweaty glands go on working profusely long after she is died). Because she has no internal organs, the only way of despatching an adult male donner is to rip off her head and limbs and skewer him through its bottom-hole with a large metall spike.

Hey listen, boysie. I remember

The Bubbelos Wipe: *Take floor cloth, and soak thoroughly in Legionnaire's disease. Trace the sacred omega sign (see below). And hey presto! – good enough for any food inspector, innit?*

sometings. Take a tip with me, OK. Someday, a geezer he will come to your shop. Watchit. He will say hallo my name Mr. Wiliams. Wrong, matey. His name spell truoble. He will say; "Hello, you want makes lots big money?"

You say: "Not if it means sleeping with a donkey."

He will say: "No. I will put this video machine in your shop and ching! ching! Bob Robinson is your Uncle, big bucks will follow."

BEWARE! He will bring in a Galaxxian machine from the taxxi ofice down the road. So. Why *they* don't want it, eh?

BECAUSE! This game she has been aroun for five maybe more year, and is easy peasy to little eihgt-year-old kids. For twenny pee they can play for hours and hours. You cannot close your bloody shop. You cannot go to your bloody bed. You cannot go to bloody sleep with your fat wife. Zap zap, on they go. They drive you a banana. Is three oclock in the bloody morning. Zap zap. Oh, here comes the milkman. Zap zap. Is time to open the bloody shop again. *These kids they no know shame!*. All they wanna do is get number one high score and print up their

name as "FART". So finally you must switch off the machine and refund the bloody money. Two bloody weeks later the electric bloody bill says "£50,000", innit?"

So, listen. Is been good talking you, boysie, keep your pecker diddlin. Tata.

BUBBELOS SALAD

£	🍷
Serves 137	
1 onion	
1 lettuce (senile)	
1 green tomato	
1 1/137th lemon	
1 cucumber (in season)	
1 dandelion (optional)	

Take the lettuce, pull off the discoloured, soggy, moldy outer leaves and place in pitta bread. Divide the tomato into generous portions, with at least three seeds in each helping. Chew the cucumber and spit out bite-size portions. Shout out something which is probably in Greek to the cook. Dice onion. By now, everything in the salad should be green. Add lemon for colour. Amend the price list with a felt tip pen. Pour ½ pint of water into pitta bread, so it collapses and salad bursts through as soon as customer lifts it out of the paper.

Shout at the funny lady with a moustache who's been drinking a cup of tea for two days. Serve.

CHIPS

£	🍷
Serves 8	
1lb flour	
1 pint water	
Fat	

Make dough in the normal way. Cut into chip shapes. Fry slightly. No-one never says nothing – try it.

"HEY, SO TELL ME, HOW YOU LIKE MY CUISINE, EH?
SHE VERY NICE GIRL VERY CHEAP,
VERY CLEAN. NOT TOO YOUNG TO MARRY, NO? OK, SO SHE
IS COVERED IN PUPPY FAT NOW, SURE,
BUT SHE CAN WASH IN THE TOILET AFTER WORK"

A la carte

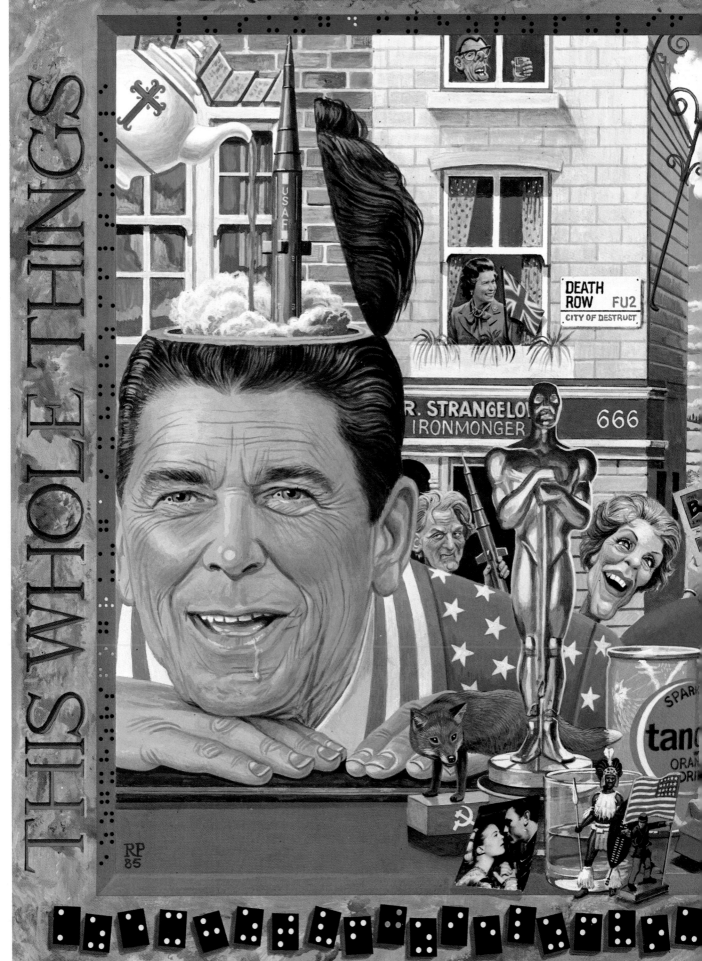

Buried somewhere in the Universe is the repulsive wrinkled item below. It is a perfect life-size replica of the President's Brain, fashioned by Luck and Flaw out of 22-carat gold, and strangely resembling a splendrous growth known as a 'walnut', oft-times used by the Ancient Egyptians to decorate their cakes.

Believe it or not, this hideous object is worth *thousands of pounds.* Faber & Faber, painfully aware that this book hasn't a paisley's chance in hell of selling on its literary merits, coughed up the necessary in an attempt to capture, as they put it, "the walnut-loving end of the market". You think they are mad. And who can blame you.

And yet, not as mad as all that, gentle browser. For anyone who is half-witted enough to want to own the ghastly thing, is hardly likely to possess the intelligence to work out how to find it. However, you are invited to try. For it is as likely to be found by the bright 33-year-old who made the puzzle up in the first place, as it is by an Oxford don.

Of all the 200 or so famous people who have appeared on Spitting Image as a puppet, only *one* knows the precise location of the gruesome medallion's tomb. If you're too bone-idle to work out the puzzle quietly and sensibly in your room, a simpler if less reliable method of winning the prize is as follows:

Wearing your Spitting Image T-shirt, accost the famous person you think it might be and, using either an electric megaphone or a rolled-up cone of cardboard, confront them loudly and insistently with the magic password:

> *Abracadee Abracadoo*
> *You are the Walnut*
> *Koo koo ke doo.*

If correctly challenged, the celebrity is sworn to reveal to you and you alone the whereabouts of the loathesome ornamento.

Dame Fortune be with you fair seeker. And remember – members of the Royal Family are addressed as Your Highness, except for the Queen who answers only to Your Majesty.

N.B. Competition not open to members of the Rolling Stones, their love-children, grand-love-children, great-grand-love-children, gophers, roadies, groupies, chauffies, buttlies, accounties, tax-consultants, stylists, nostril-surgeons, governesses, arse-lickers, houseboys, publicists, bouncers, masseuses, food-tasters, managers, under-managers or management trainees. Competition opens on 7th October 1985.

Benendover's School for Boys

THE FALOPIAN

PER SCHOLARE AD STOCKEXCHANGEO

Governors

Mr. A. Banker
His Worship A. Bishop
Sir A. General
Mr. A. N. Old Boy
Joanna Lumley

Headmaster — Roger Branston-Pickle
Head Boy — Nigel Branston-Pickle

FROM THE HEADMASTER

Once again we come to the end of another year. Another year of successes and failures in the endless round of the academic whirl! Where can I start? Well at least we avoided a flu epidemic which usually hits us in the Easter Term but we might be considered a touch unlucky to have had a major outbreak of the killer disease AIDS. The sanatorium certainly came into its own with the 257 reported cases. Well done Matron! This may have accounted for the somewhat disappointing performance in the examination results. Some parents might feel that 4 CSE Woodwork passes in the whole Sixth Form is a little below average for a school charging £15,000 per annum. Let me remind them again that it is not only academic results that count in the making of a Falopian but an all-round education that is, fortunately, impossible to define. For example on the Sportsfield the school lived up to its motto: "It's not the winning, it's the taking part that counts". And we certainly took part this year. So as we say farewell to Falopians who are passing on to a better life, and of course to those who are leaving the school, I hope that their days here will be remembered as the most profitable of their lives. They certainly have been in my case.

Quentin Crispimas Term

Appeal Fund

Yes we made it!! Last year's appeal reached its target of £100,000 thanks to the generosity of parents, staff, pupils and old boys. Well done everyone! Three cheers! The money came from covenants, donations, gifts and a fair bit of embezzling by the Bursar – well done him! On July 4th this year the Branston-Pickle Memorial Swimming Pool, Jacuzzi and Sauna was officially opened by the Headmaster's wife, Mrs Branston-Pickle, in the grounds of the Headmaster's House. The pool complex can now be enjoyed by all, young and old alike, who live in the Headmaster's House. The plans for the New Music School and Library, detailed in the Appeal Brochure, have had to be temporarily shelved due to the inflationary cost of the New Swimming Pool. This year we're asking you to dig even deeper into your pockets, to raise the £120,000 needed urgently to get the popular form master of the under 14's, Mr Nepis, out of jail. As soon as this bail can be raised Mr Nepis will be rejoining the staff and the boys to whom he has become so attached over the years. Please make your cheques payable to The Nepis Appeal, c/o PIE Box 31, LONDON. Thanks again.

Under 14's Rugby

Mr Nepis is very keen to take over and is replacing Mr Jones as from next term.

ROGER BRANSTON–PICKLE
(Headmaster)

NEWS OF OLD BOYS

M J V Beanoe (D House Master 1937–39) has just retired as Colonial Officer for Lower Zimbabwe District Office. He is retiring to Guildford and would like to get in touch with any old boys who remember the pillow fights in D Dorm. He is very sad.

P R F Troosers (F House 1942–47) is now working in the Foreign Office and would like to get in touch with any of the under 14 Rugby Squad who might be interested in scouting and amateur photography.

P F L Urne (G House 1903–1907) Has been dead for 14 years, but would like to get in touch with any old boys who are mediums.

The School Play

WE did "Oliver" this year, marking the 20th anniversary of the First School Production of "Oliver" and making it 20 years on the trot that the school has chosen to perform the play. Mr Nepis played Nancy, as he has done since the first show and this year gave a memorable performance, remembering nearly all his lines. Few of us will forget his heartrending rendition of "Old Man River". There was a praiseworthy performance from Perkins as the Artful Dodger, and it is a shame that he has since been expelled for stealing from the tuckshop. Roberts Major was a splendid Oliver, perhaps a baritone being an odd choice, and the whole was brilliantly directed by the Headmaster who asked me to write this review. A play is not just the actors and special thanks must go to Mr Cripps of the carpentry department whose magnificent set held up so admirably for the first half. Great fun was had by the make-up department under Mr Nepis who all decided to make themselves up as Chinese Call Girls. Still, all good clean fun and we look forward to next years play, "Oliver", with bated breath!!

R Jones
(Classics Master)

A TRIBUTE TO HARRY "KIPPER" RAGWORM

It is with heavy heart that I must relate the death of Harry "Kipper" Ragworm, the classics master, at the early age of 107. "Kipper" was teaching right until the end and died as he would like to have done "whilst caning a small boy for having his hands in his pockets during a half-day holiday". Harry and his trustworthy collection of canes were well known to generations of Falopians and many an old boy will remember being flogged to within an inch of his life for coughing during Chapel. "Kipper" had taught continuously at this school ever since 1903 with a short sabbatical between 1953 and 1973 after a best forgotten incident involving the death at his hands of a junior third former for whistling in the corridor. This apart, "Kipper" had an impossible record as an unorthodox classics master, knowing no Greek or Latin at all. He was much loved by no one.

POEMS

APPLE
One bite
And angels wept.
One fruit
Was all it took
Sin was upon us
Oh no.
A garden of Eden lost for ever
EVER
Think about that when
You smoke behind the bike sheds

A Blackwood (12) 4th Form

Fall
Fall
Fall

Bombs
Bombs falling from the sky
Mushroom War,
A nuclear child cries:
"We are the lost men"
Who listens to the
Hymn of the Dead?
As the Bombs fall

C Gunness (13)
Lower 4th

Snakes are long and slimy like in school toilets and live J Feroze (11) 2nd Form

THE LOVE THAT DARE NOT DECLARE ITS NAME

Oh Leslie
My love, My only.
Let us throw caution to the wind
My child
And declare our oneness
To the uncomprehending world
Who dare say our love is wrong?
We know
And that is all there is in the
Joy of Union.

MR Nepis (52) Pentonville

SUPER NEW PRACTICAL JOKES AND WHEEZES from BOFFO'S JOKE CATALOGUE

FAKE PERIOD POOL Amaze your friends and have them *screaming* with laughter. Just leave the plastic fake "pool" under a girl's chair, and watch her face as she *rushes* off to the lav!!

"RUNOVER" GRANNY Place fake plastic squashed grandmother under the wheels of Pop's car. Stand back and wait for *hilarious* results.

REAL "FAKE" GUN Looks like a gun cigarette lighter, but is in fact a *real* gun. Offer a chum a light, and when he pulls the trigger, try and stop yourself *guffawing* as the bullet takes the top of his head off!

BRAIN TUMOUR POWDER Simply slip some into a friend's coffee – within *minutes* his brain will haemorrhage!!

The Lady

Est. 1885
Vol. 201 No. 5216

Editorial

A word from Our Leader Herself . . .

'Get out of my way, you little pratts.'

Teachers' Rights

By Sir Keith Joseph

Once again, the teachers' unions are badgering for a pay rise. Their argument is that the living standard of teachers has dropped dramatically over the Tory term of office. But just how true is this? In 1979 the average teacher drove a Citroen 2cv, with a "Nuclear Power – No Thanks" sticker on the windscreen, wore tweedy jackets with leather patches on the elbows, brown corduroy trousers, drank 145 cups of coffee per day, and smoked a pipe. He was nicknamed "Homo" or "Inky", depending on his surname, and drank 3½ pints of beer every evening. He acted like "one of the lads" with the upper sixth form, which was odd, because only three years earlier he'd been pulling their ears for talking at lunch-time, and making them stand in the corner for giggling. He was incapable of mixing with other adults, because he constantly lapsed into that patronising impatience that a lifetime of ordering little people around produces. He was very interested in wood-stripping or D-I-Y or anything, really, to fill that yawning hollowness in his life. He was a sad, unenviable character, whose ultimate ambition was to live in an Alan Ayckbourne play, where everybody thought he was witty. And, as far as I can see, the same applies today. Which rather knocks a hole in their contention, or I'm a Chinaman.

Howe on Finance

Sir Geoffrey Howe recalls his term as Chancellor of the Exchequer

DID YOU KNOW that the annual rate of inflation in Argentina is in excess of 1000%? That means if you buy a chocolate bar in January for ten pee, by December, it would cost £10, and then, a year later, it would fetch a princely £100, which is a bit stiff, really, considering it's almost certain to have gone off by then.

Anyway, the point is, it's about time we put those Johnny Gouchos in their place, and I've persuaded my bank manager to draft them a rather stiff letter, which should put the wind right up their greasy spic hides.

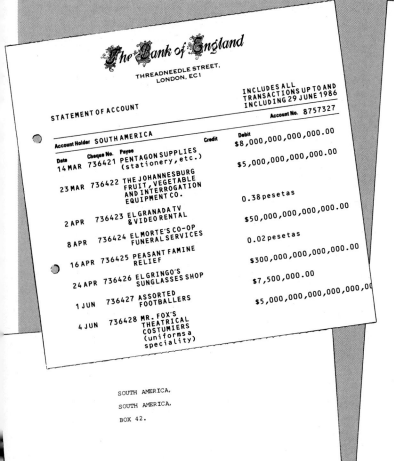

The Bank of England

THREADNEEDLE STREET,
LONDON, EC1

STATEMENT OF ACCOUNT

INCLUDES ALL TRANSACTIONS UP TO AND INCLUDING 29 JUNE 1986

Account No. 8757327

Account Holder SOUTH AMERICA			Credit	Debit
Date	Cheque No.	Payee		
14 MAR	736421	PENTAGON SUPPLIES (stationery, etc.)		$8,000,000,000,000.00
23 MAR	736422	THE JOHANNESBURG FRUIT, VEGETABLE AND INTERROGATION EQUIPMENT CO.		$5,000,000,000,000.00
2 APR	736423	EL GRANADA TV & VIDEO RENTAL	0.38 pesetas	
8 APR	736424	EL MORTE'S CO-OP FUNERAL SERVICES		$50,000,000,000,000.00
16 APR	736425	PEASANT FAMINE RELIEF	0.02 pesetas	
24 APR	736426	EL GRINGO'S SUNGLASSES SHOP		$300,000,000,000,000.00
1 JUN	736427	ASSORTED FOOTBALLERS		$7,500,000.00
4 JUN	736428	MR. FOX'S THEATRICAL COSTUMIERS (uniforms a speciality)		$5,000,000,000,000,000,00

SOUTH AMERICA,
SOUTH AMERICA,
BOX 42.

The Bank of England

THREADNEEDLE STREET,
LONDON, EC1

SOUTH AMERICA,
SOUTH AMERICA,
BOX 42,

29th June 1986

Dear South America,

It has come to our attention that you are now £5,000 million billion overdrawn on your current account.

According to our records, there is no arrangement for an overdraft of this size, which, you will concede, exceeds the agreed £100 limit.

If you would like to arrange an appointment with the sub-manager, Mr. Harding, he will be pleased to discuss any problems you have managing your account.

In the meantime, we must ask you to cease using your cheque card forthwith. We must also warn you that, should you attempt to use the cash dispenser in Rio de Janeiro, it will retain your card.

I'm afraid we have been obliged to refuse to honour your two most recent cheques: one to El Hombra's Discount Liquor Store for 27 pesetas, and the other to International Technical Marketing Services Ltd (Weapons) for the sum of £100,000,000. Should you make funds available and re-present the cheques, we shall be happy to honour them.

I enclose a statement of your account,

Yours faithfully,

(Manager)

The Lady

THE TORY PARTY IN-HOUSE MAGAZINE
(Incorporating Toadying Today)

APRIL 1985

NOUVELLE CUISINE DU DHSS

BY TOM KING (EMPLOYMENT MINISTER)

*S*ardine avec Sauce Rouge et Sauce Brun

We all know how hard it is to live in style on the dole on £28.43 a week. Well, I don't, of course, but somehow, my great-grandfather managed it in 1860, and it's still possible today given a little imagination, careful budgeting, and the ability to commit grand theft without getting caught.

Nouvelle cuisine is a posh and expensive way of not having very much to eat. However, it is possible to create a reasonable facsimile on a shoestring, so that you, the Backbone Of The Country (poor people) can eat like the rich (me). Yes, it *is* possible to enjoy food without serving a hundred and forty pounds of potatoes mashed in dripping every meal, you horrible oiks.

Above are some suggested recipes which are cheap, attractive, and guaranteed to produce groans of incredulous delight in Canal Street, Bog End, or whatever miserable old working-class terraced ho(use) vel you live in where the neighbours are always arguing in the street.

*D*igit de Poisson avec Pommes de Terre et Krona

Given this start, and your own dreary imagination, you'll be able to pass off any old twaddle as nouvelle cuisine to that wretched old ricket-ridden son of a ferret fancier you married, poor sod. String beans, using real string, or Cor-nish pasty with genuine corns. How about a tasty cardboard pâté, or some chilled frog-wart soup? Goldfish droppings, rolled up and chilled can taste deceptively like caviare. And what about the children? A small baby can make a deliciously crunchy little meal for eight, and you probably wouldn't even miss him.

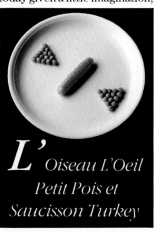

*L'*Oiseau L'Oeil Petit Pois et Saucisson Turkey

*S*paghetti sec à la Kit-e-kat

campain

A Heseltine potboiler   22 Jeremy 1983   only 70p reduced to clear

ARBLM grabs £3m J & Q slice from BHP

In a shock move last week, top agency Ambrose, Rolfe, Butt, Lemming and Mayhew (ARBLM) scooped £3m worth of Billings from top tobacco retailer, J & Q. J & Q were rumoured to have moved the account due to "dissatisfaction" with creative hot house, Bogleby, Hargell and Pratt (BHP) who were responsible for the poster campaign (see above). J & Q claimed there was a high degree of "Brand Confusion" over the campaign promoting their new filter tip cigarettes, 'Satin Slits'.

Creative director Paul Pratt told *Campain*: "That's nonsense. My campaign has been a brilliant success and has put the name 'Silk Cut' on the lips of . . . sorry that should be 'Satin Slits' on the lips of every man woman and child in the country."

ARBLM + P lose £3m J & Q slice to Wright Gitt and Rutherford

In a shock move yesterday tobacco giant J & Q moved its £3m account to W G and R, the small breakaway go ahead agency, famous for its directors' bow ties and silly plastic glasses. A J & Q spokesman said of its previous agency, ARBLM+P, "We went to them for something fresh and original and all they came up with was a picture of cloth with holes in it. People still think we're 'Silk Cut'."

A tight-lipped Paul Pratt commented: "There is no confusion what so ever between 'Silk Slits' and Satin Cut."

Bogleby, Hargell and Pratt lose £3m J&Q slice to ARBLM

In a shock move last week top creative hot house BHP lost its prize £3m J & Q slice to ARBLM (See identical story left). A spokesman for J & Q, producers of the new cigarettes, 'Satin Slits', said: "We feel the campaign, though effective and not at all a complete waste of money, has in many ways been free advertising for 'Silk Cut', our well known competitor."

A tight lipped Paul Pratt commented: "There has been no confusion whatsoever between 'Silk Slits' and 'Satin Cuts'. They are two completely different products about as similar, if I may say so, as chalk and . . . a completely different kind of chalk." Mr Pratt refused to comment further and when asked about his future with Bogleby, Hargell and Pratt, said "Make no mistake. I am here to stay."

ARBLM welcomes Pratt from Bogleby Hargell

Paul Pratt has moved to become creative director of top agency ARBLM, now to be known as ARBLM and P. "It's great to be working with such a brilliant creative team who work 10% harder than anyone else. Their integrity shines through their advertising and I'm proud to be associated with them." he said. His first job is to come up with a new design for the prestigious J & Q tobacco account for its new product 'Satin Slits'. Pratt said: "I want to do something fresh and original, but I'm not letting on what the theme will be ."

Pratt fired from ARBLM

Paul Pratt is to leave ARBLM due to what he called "a difference in managerial styles." He told *Campain*: "This has nothing to do with 'Slit Cuts' advertisements which I freely admit were a disaster but which were entirely the fault of everyone else." "In fact", he continued "I have every good reason to believe a certain giant tobacco company will transfer their account to whichever company I join next."

In a shock move . . .

In a shock move, Wright Gitt and Rutherford welcomed Paul Pratt as their new creative boss and immediately lost the prized J & Q tobacco account. Pratt told *Campain* "There is no connection between the two events at all. I'm definitely here to stay." However a J & Q spokesman commented: "We couldn't believe it. That guy Pratt turned up in a bow tie and glasses and showed us his new design. It centred round a piece of linen with a tear in it." The business has now gone to agency Bogleby and Hargell who Pratt described as "A real bunch of cowboys if ever I saw one."

Pratt fired from Bogleby Hargell and Pratt

Paul Pratt, creative director of the hot house, Bogleby, Hargell and Pratt, has left the agency due to what he calls "creative differences": – "I felt limited by what I could achieve at BHP and needed to expand my personal horizons." When asked if his departure had anything to do with the 'Satin Slits' advertisement, he replied: "Not at all. I agree that it was a disastrous campaign but that was entirely the fault of Bogleby and Hargell who are complete idiots. I kept suggesting that there was some similarity but they would not listen to me. There is no acrimony though."

Wright Gitt and Rutherford grab £3m J & Q slice from ARBLM and P

Top breakaway agency W G and R has landed the prized £3m J & Q account from top agency ARBLM and P. A J & Q spokesman said "We were particularly impressed with their record, their bow ties and their plastic spectacles." Paul Pratt, creative head of losing agency ARBLM+P said: "This is a shoddy move from a shoddy agency and is typical of W G and R." Once again Pratt defended his campaign saying: "There was no confusion between 'Silk Satins' and 'Cut Silks.'"

PLEAT BELLENHOLE with Tony Jacklin

OPEN SHOULDERS. STAND WELL BACK FROM THE BALL. HIT INTO AND ALONG THE LINE, ALLOWING THE LOFT OF THE CLUB FACE TO PERFORM ITS' NATURAL FUNCTION OF GETTING THE BALL IN THE AIR.

THUD!

AH, MUST HAVE MISJUDGED MY BACKSWING. REMEMBER CORRECT TIMING BETWEEN LEGS, BODY & HANDS IS ABSOLUTELY VITAL... ...AHG

SPLUT!!

SORRY, BIT OF A WHILE SINCE I LAST PLAYED. MOST OF MY TIME DOING PROMOTIONS. ONLY USED TO BE ABLE TO DO THIS AND I WOULDN'T WANT ANYONE TO THINK I WAS JUST ANOTHER OLD BORING HAS BEEN WHO'S...

TAKE THAT YOU ROTTEN LITTLE SOD

NO-ONE LOOKING ARE THEY. RIGHT

...LOOK! KNOW WHAT YOU'RE THINKING BUT I AM A VERY FAMOUS GOLFER AND I DID WIN THE BRITISH AND AMERICAN OPENS IN 1969. OR WAS IT 1971. EVEN THOUGH PEOPLE UNDER SEVENTEEN STARE BLANKLY IF YOU MENTION MY NAME.

ON THE LOST PLANET OF BLATANT SYMBOLISM AXA MEETS THE DREADED TROUSER-SNAKE.....

COZ NO-ONE'S INTERESTED IN SCI-FI DARLIN' — DROP 'EM!!!

OH NO! WHY HAVE ALL MY CLOTHES FALLEN OFF?!

A X A

RUPERT

"What's wrong?" asked Rupert. "It's you," said Bill. "You're a stodgy old middle-class, middle-aged conservative who still believes in a world that disappeared thirty years ago."
"That's right," agreed Daddy. "Just like the Daily Express!"

STAR QUICK BRAIN TEASER

What is the next number in the sequence?

1, 2, 3, 4, 5, 6, 7, 8, 9, 10, 11, 12, 13, 14, 15, 16, 17, 18, 19, 20, 21, 22, 23, 24, 25, 26, 27, 28, 29, 30, 31, 32, 33, 34, 35, 36, 37, 38, 39, 40, 41, 42, 43, 44, 45,

SPITTING IMAGE SECRETS

Q: Why do we always get at Donald Sinden so much?

A: Don't know.

FOR YOUR SPECIAL DAY...

Your wedding day should be the most perfect day of your entire life. And no wedding reception is complete without OBNOXIOUS RELATIVES. If you haven't got any, why not hire some from us?

There is a vast selection available:

Disgraceful lecherous uncle

Moaning old biddy who won't stop talking about her feet

Loud and brash kids – selection of three. (Dog-torturing a speciality)

Eight-month-old baby who cries through the hymns and poos loudly during the vows

Dangerous long-lost cousin (knives provided)

Vomiting grandparents (48 hours notice)

Also – for your musical entertainment – Obnoxious D.J. who speaks American with a Salford accent, and spends all night long, and plays "The Birdie Song" impressing all the 14-year-old girls who think he's in showbusiness.

Rancid
WEDDING HIRE

Really Useful Requiems Ltd (in association with EMI Records) are proud to present Andrew Lloyd Webber's **P.A.Y.E. JESU** with

KYRIE T. KANALAGA
PLACEBO FLAMINGO
A SMALL BOY

With lyrics by Jo Zanna, Doris Irae. Rex Tremendae.

WHAT THE CRITICS SAY:

"The rock music section is wonderful"
The Classical Music Press

"The classical bits are wonderful"
The Rock Music Press

"The lyrics are crap"
Richard Stilgoe

"The crap is wonderful"
Tim Rice

Stay out of the limelight whilst staying *in* the exhaust fumes!

SINCLAIR C5 OWNER DRIVERS ACCESSORY KIT

CONSISTS:

Wig, false beard, dark glasses, ex-Special Branch Assault balaclava (choice of thicknesses).

Be the laughing stock of your friends, don't buy one

Send £2.50 + 60p p&p now to: The Master O'Disguise, Hattersley Trading Park, Hovis New Town, Gwent.

JOKES JOKES

DOGGY POO-POO

Place on the side of plate at dinner, looks just like real doggy poo. When you pick it up you find... it is!

THE REALLY REALLY SICK JOKE SHOP
MAXWELL AVENUE
STOKE-ON-DRUGS

TODAY'S THOUGHT

"When I take my clothes off, I look like Mr Toad of Toad Hall." WILLIAM SHATNER (CAPT. KIRK T. J. HOOKER)

DEAD Letters ●●●●●

ENORMOUS PUN TO FILL SPACE

Dear Old Pair,

DO blind people masturbate? My wife says they do but I'm not so sure. If they do, what do they think about? (I am a registered blind person, so this letter isn't in poor taste or anything).

Yours, Reg Collins.

(Reg by name and Reg by nature!)

★ Couldn't say Reg, off the cuff! We were always told that it happened the other way round: that you went blind AFTER you masturbated.

OLD SONG

Dear Old Codgers,

MY wife says that Andrew Lloyd Webber's 'Midnight' from 'Cats' is the same tune as Ravel's 'Bolero'. Our marriage is now on the rocks. Can you Old Pair help?

★ No PUSSYFOOTING around! She's right. Maurice Ravel (1875-1937) was a great admirer of Andrew Lloyd Webber's stage works. His other admirers include Britten, Elgar, Mendelssohn, Fauré, Verdi, Holst and every single music critic in the country, sir.

Write to us Old Codgers

Our address is:

The Young Trainee Smartasses, Daily Turd, 489, Fleet Street, London EC1PX3QQR

We regret no letters can be returned or indeed read as we are too busy making them up

THE THINGS KIDS SAY!

MY six-year-old nephew had been playing in the garden. After a while he came in and asked me what a wasp was. I told him it was a black and yellow flying insect whose wings make a buzzing sound. Quick as a flash he replied, grinning impishly, "so it's a bit like a

OVERHEARD ON A BUS

"How much is it to Marble Arch?"
"Fifty, Love"
"Ta', Love"
"Ta, love.

Slimmer OF THE YEAR

ELIZABETH TAYLOR writes

Can you believe that just a year ago I weighed 280lbs? (175 without jewellery).

Yes, I had a weight problem, but I didn't admit it until the day my agent said the role of Moby Dick was mine, if I could lose twenty lbs. About the same time, I started to notice men passing me in the street without giving me so much as a second marriage.

I had to do something. *Fast!* (Or maybe just diet...) I treated myself to one last binge and went out and ate a Macdonald's (and a French restaurant.)

The next day I began my regime. I made a rule never to eat between mouthfuls or when I was asleep. I tried going out without my fridge. I had only lo-calorie food at my wedding receptions. But the weight stayed on.

Desperate measures were called for. Three of my ex-husbands were sweet enough to arrange for my jaws to be clamped together – nothing elaborate, just a little diamond clip from Cartier's. But before long I had the knack of pushing bananas up my nose, and pouring the cream into my ear.

Then, at last, salvation! I got admitted to the Betty Ford Clinic. Believe me, the flab just fell off. I came out looking almost gaunt and haggard. I'd recommend anyone to spend three months in the company of Liza Minelli.

TIT

The Sun regrets that due to industrial action by the National Association of Wheezing Gits and Allied Communist Skivers we are unable to print photographs in today's super paper

---

LUDICROUS COOT ON POETRY

this mild winter positively must attract daylightsaving timebeguiling interlopers   by tseliott

ingenious ptolemaic charts
indivisible piteous hearts
egotistical immoralinvisible foolishness
propitious cities
tattered cryptochristian tinkercarts

Kingsley Amis writes: "I'm shorry I've abbsolutely no shodding idea what thish ish all about. Apparently Tennyshon (or wash it Keatsh?) wash having a dreem when shome chappie from Plympton rushshed in, wrote thish lode of cobblersh on hish jotter and rushshed out again. When Byron (or Me or whoeveritwas) woke up they died from Opium poishoning.

Where Like A Train My Truelove Goes
by Robert Maxwell (1809-)

The trouble with Solzhenitsyn Is his books have got no titsyn.

Robert Maxwell is not only a Colossus of Twentieth Century Literature, he is also standing Immediately Behind Me.

◄ EROTIC NIGHTWEAR

HIS: Flannelette pyjamas with ridiculous gaping hole. For the man who likes to dangle.
HERS: "Demis Roussos" clinging top, with stiletto Doctor Marten's boots and 'hairy leg' effect stockings.
RUDE CLOTHES: £25 per set or 1 week at £25.00

£25.00

£24.99

◄ THE CECIL PARKINSON EX-SECRETARY WASTEBIN.

BIN: £24.99 or 40 days and 40 nights at £5.34

► LINEN AFTER SHAVE/ EAU DE COLOGNE

With the irresistible fragrance, for the man who doesn't know what the hell he's up to.
GIFT SET: £1.30 or 53 weeks at £1.29

£7.30

► DEATH IN THE POLICE CELL

A new murder mystery game. Can you find Whodunnit? Ages 8 to 80.
GAME: £7.95 or 23456 weeks at 4 doubloons

£7.95

£6.50

◄ THE LEONARD NIMOY "SERIOUS ACTOR" KIT

Featuring Mr. Spock ears. **"To boldly go, or not to boldly go – that is the silly actor kit": £6.50 or 100 Federation Credits.**

£5.00

◄ LORD LUCAN MARITAL AID

Enhance your sex life with one of our super range of "Famous Faces" sheaths. Also in Andrew Lloyd Webber and Desmond Wilcox styles.
LATEX JONATHON: £5 per pack of 5 or 54 weeks at £1,000,000

► FRIDGE/FREEZER

With handy Russian Leader compartment.
REFRIGERATOR: 56,000,000 roubles or 345 weeks at 5 kopeks

56000000 roubles

► CHEAP AND NASTY ELECTRIC ORGAN

Just plug it in, and within seconds you'll be sounding exactly like an asthmatic with a collapsed lung playing a plastic harmonica. Includes music tutor "PLAY IN A DAY, THE JIM 'JOANNA' CALLAGHAN WAY." (Featuring "Skip to the loo, before the bag bursts" and "Will ye no talk proper?"
ORGAN: £0.56 or 53 weeks at £12.54

£0.56

£15.50

◄ TOP OF THE POPS DEEJAY OUTFIT

Now you can pretend you're a completely talentless old fart the BBC are too feckless to get rid of! Comes complete with wheelchair, microphone, scaffolding and cut-out jailbait, with a manual on how to use the word "Excellent" as many times as possible*.

*Peter Powell version only
AGEING HIPPY KIT: £15.50 or 12 years at 25% of your income

£25.95

◄ JUNIOR "BOY GEORGE" OUTFIT

With free bottom-widener.
GENDER BENDER KIT: £25.95 (Wig, hat and make-up not included)

► PORTABLE TELEVISION

With blank screen and no sound, so you can watch Channel Four even if the Pope drops in for a bath.
TV: £165, or 52 weeks at £20.99

£165.00

THE LANCET

No 7345   LONG WEEKEND 8-22 MAY 1978   VOL 5 FOR 1978

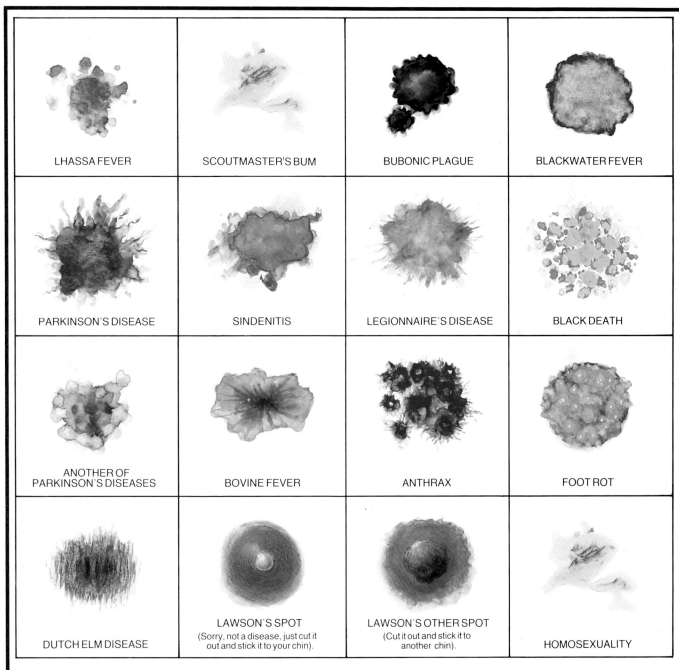

LHASSA FEVER   SCOUTMASTER'S BUM   BUBONIC PLAGUE   BLACKWATER FEVER

PARKINSON'S DISEASE   SINDENITIS   LEGIONNAIRE'S DISEASE   BLACK DEATH

ANOTHER OF PARKINSON'S DISEASES   BOVINE FEVER   ANTHRAX   FOOT ROT

DUTCH ELM DISEASE

LAWSON'S SPOT
(Sorry, not a disease, just cut it out and stick it to your chin).

LAWSON'S OTHER SPOT
(Cut it out and stick it to another chin).

HOMOSEXUALITY

SCRATCH 'n' CATCH

A unique opportunity to contract some of the world's greatest diseases. To contract similar diseases would cost thousands of pounds in air fares alone. Now exclusive to readers of the Lancet we are able to offer the chance to catch all these diseases for FREE! Imagine that, enjoy the pleasure of the world's greatest known diseases, in the comfort of your own home!!!

WHAT TO DO
Simply rub your thumb or forefinger (other organs may not work) across the sample of bacteria indicated below. Alternatively rub your food across the page and consume.
If symptoms persist consult your local doctor immediately and ask for individual 'private' care.

H DIGNITY

If you're too embarrassed to take your hat off in the bath, voraciously read articles by Duncan Goodhew, and take a manly pride in exhibiting your nostril-hairs at flower shows or growing a beard, you may be on the road to baldness with dignity

Paul Sample

W ho wants to wear a toupee? Who wants a swoop, or even a double swoop?

There is an alternative – the Decoy Theory. Growing a beard distracts attention from the balding pate, especially if it's one of those big black mormon-type beards, with tomato soup stains around the mouth and bits of crisps and bamboo shoots lurking in the luxuriant growth.

But why stop there?

There are many ways of distracting the gaze away from the cranium, without losing your dignity. For instance, constantly walking around with your flies open and wearing moose antlers.

Mixing stripes and checks is always an eye-catcher. Especially if you mix them on the same pair of trousers. Musical ties and big floppy clown shoes with fluorescent flashing lights are not only dignified, but look good, too. Carrying a rotting herring under your arm is guaranteed to produce a non-hair-loss conversation. There are many small adjustments to your physiognomy that are cheap, painless and produce the desired effect. Wooden den-

tures. Metal ears. An eye-patch is always a good stand-by. Particularly effective if worn over the mouth.

The Decoy Theory is not new. Long John Silver was a prime exponent. Who would ever dream of remarking on his baldness, when he went around with a wooden leg, a crutch, an eye-patch, a parrot on his shoulder, a silly hat, and only washed between Transatlantic voyages? No sir. Long John Silver achieved the ambition of every coot: baldness with dignity.

BALDNESS WIT

Ambitious new styles

THE SWOOP

For years, this has been the popular solution to disguising baldness without wearing a wig. The simple expedient of growing the hair on the side of your head, back of your neck, armpit, etc., then swooping it over and plastering it down with Cossack or Evostick.

THE DOUBLE SWOOP

Similar to the swoop, except the hair is grown 2 to 3 feet longer, so that, when it's swept over, it will cover not only your own head, but the head of a bald companion.

THE TOPIARY CHICKEN

The notion here is that your hair looks nothing like real hair, therefore you can't possibly be wearing a toupee. Also in Windmill and Rampant Griffin shapes.

BALD SPOT

In his lifetime, Casanova made love to a reputed 35,000 women! He wasn't bald – but he did get syphilis and died horribly. Ha!

THE CUCKOO'S NEST

Darken the rims of your eyes with mascara pencil, adopt vacant expression, and stick two fake lobotomy scars on your forehead. No one will dare remark on your hair-loss because they'll believe you're recovering from major brain surgery. Dribbling saliva and muttering at people who aren't there caps the image, and enables you to blend naturally in any social group. (*Note: A bonus here* – Any odd behaviour on your part will pass without comment. Sporting this style, I once goosed every woman at a society party, and stole their 3-piece suite)

WIG TEST

Mike Roosevelt takes the new Franklin GTi super-toupee out for a spin.

The first thing you notice about the Franklin is it's a convertible.

If you get bored with one side, just flip it over for a new colour and a new style. It's even got a sun roof – a small bald patch you can remove in the summer. The zip's not fantastic – but who cares with a wig this authentic-looking?

First stop – the shower. I stood under the running water for 15 minutes, and didn't get wet. Water absorption – excellent.

Now for the big test – how would it compare with real hair out on the street?

Laden as it was with water, it didn't corner very well. I found if I turned my head too swiftly, the Franklin would stay firmly in its original position, and I'd be left with a sideburn down the front of my nose.

The measure of a toupee is when you forget you're wearing it. And I certainly found this with the Franklin. Until I realised that, because of the weight of the water, I'd started walking like Groucho Marx.

All in all, a sporty, young executive model. The suction pads provide excellent adhesion, though they do tend to leave ugly red rings, and are slightly harder to remove than the tightest-fitting riding boots. You'll probably need a little help to get it off. Your wife or girl friend with a foot in between your shoulder blades should do it. Or better still, a Range Rover with a grappling hook (a tow bar comes as standard on the Franklin). And the good news – once it had dried out, shrinkage on the Franklin was less than 50%. Highly recommended.

BALD SPOT

TV Actor Telly Savalas is bald. He is also hideously ugly. He is also Greek. Poor guy.

16

CUSTOM HAIR

POLICE INFORMATION GAZETTE

INCORPORATING Amateur Moustache-grower & Masonic News.   No. 999

60p (UK Black Market)

EDITORIAL

By Detective Sergeant Norris Dimbleby of the Met.

'Ello?

BRAIN-TEEZER

Can you match wits with Inspector Basterd?
A man is found hanging in his cell, by a pair of police braces. He has a truncheon embedded in his right ear.
The cell door was locked from the inside.
No-one was seen entering or leaving, except for five Police Officers putting their jackets back on, and saying "Who says the Death Penalty has been abolished? Har har har."
What was Inspector Basterd's verdict?
(Ans. below)

ON THE BEAT

1. STOP

2. GET OUT OF THE CAR

3. ARE YOU A MASON?

4. THAT'S ALL RIGHT THEN.
MIND HOW YOU GO, SIR.

GARDENING TIPS

Plant early, not later on when people are watching.
P.C. "Greenfingers" Filthe.

SOLUTION: Death by misadventure.
BRAIN-TEEZER

'POLICE ARE STUPID' CLAIM SENSATION

In a sensational outburst this week, the Magazine "Strange Thingies", dismissed a top police officer as "thick", "stupid" and "possessed of an intellectual capacity more commonly associated with pond-life invisible to the naked eye".

We of the Police Information Gazette do not wish to dignify these allegations with a denial. Instead, we re-print in full the interview on which the Magazine based its claim . . .

The Police have been using psychics in particularly difficult investigations for years, claims Det Sgt Dimbleby of the Met: "If we get particularly stuck, we're not averse to bringing in a psychic or two, although this is not officially recognised".

"Personally, I think they're a bit mad. And I've always been sceptical, but you can't argue with results. If you want someone duffing up, bring in a psychic. If confessions are a bit thin on the ground, a psychic can always extract one for you. The SPG is full of . . ."

Didn't he mean "psychos"?
"Yes".

Didn't he know I was from the paranormal magazine "Strange Thingies" and wanted to talk about psychics?
"Oh".

What about psychics, mediums, people with ESP and telekinetic abilities, did the police ever use *them*?
"Yeah. If they're handy with their fists."

SPOT • THE • DIFFERENCE

GUILTY BLACK MAN   **INNOCENT BLACK MAN**

SOLUTION: Trick question – there is no difference.

SMALL ADS

FOR SALE: Police Helmet. Covered some of Erica Roe's left breast at Twickenham. Never washed. £40, or will swap for Ronald McDonald balloon. BOX 345

Police Computer. As used in Yorkshire Ripper investigation. £1.99. Or will swap for really nice whistle.

One book. Unused. Green. Will swap for one with pictures.

PROMOTIONS

PC Wibblecleme has been promoted to Commander of the entire Thames Valley Police, a jump of 38 ranks. Our congratulations to Commander Wibblecleme who is married. Hobbies include wearing aprons and rolling up his trouser leg. He is a popular, down-to-earth copper, known to his mates as "The Grand Worshipful Master of the Knights of the Temple Rouge".

NICE 'N' NASTY agony column

Dear NICE 'N' NASTY,
We have three children and a happy home. But recently I have become convinced my wife is having an affair with my brother. I am heartbroken, as I love her dearly, and would do anything to keep our marriage together. What can I do? I'm at my wit's end.

Yours, Troubled

NICE COP I know just how you feel. You've had a rotten time, but, if you're willing to forgive, and talk it through with . . .

NASTY COP Nah! Let me at him, George. I'll soon have him singing a different tune.

NICE COP Come on, Sid – can't you see he's been having a 'ard time?

NASTY Bollocks. He's a villain. Give us five minutes alone with him. We'll soon find out if he did the Jewellers or not.

NICE Look here – I'm trying to help, but there's not a lot I can do unless you co-operate a bit. So why don't you come clean, and save yourself a lot . . .

NASTY No deals, George. I want him sent down for the full stretch. We're talking 15 years, Sunshine. And what d'you think your missus is going to get up to while you're inside? 'Er and your brother – They'll be at it hammer and tongues – *in your bed!* Come to think of it I might call round myself.

NICE Lay off him Sid. Fag, son? Look, let's have a nice cup of tea, and talk about you signing this document 'ere, then we can all get a bit of shut-eye.

NASTY Which is more than your missus'll be doing. Open all hours, eh? We never close.

NICE That's enough, Sid. You're going too far . . . don't . . . Don't . . . **DON'T!!!**

NASTY Sorry, George. Sometimes I get a bit carried away. Nasty fall you've had there, son.

We were delighted to receive this follow-up letter from our correspondent, who had taken our good advice to heart:

Dear Nice Cop,
Yes, yes. I confess I did the jewellers. Anything – just keep that animal away from me. I also wish 385 other offences which you can't clear off your books to be taken into consideration. Please, please can I go to sleep now. He won't come back, will he? That big guy?
Ahhhhhhh. . . .

Troubled.

CARTOONS

HOT DOG!

This month's celebrity centrefold is **HRH Prince Andrew.**

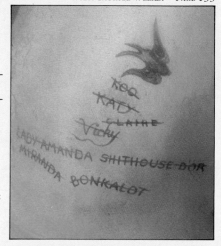

Andy is by far the dishiest Royal, not having inherited many of the genetic disorders which mar the royal bloodline. Not for him the hump of Richard III, nor the babbling insanity of Canute, but rather the legendary genitalia of Cuthbert the Ploughman (815-820) who, according to legend, left a small furrow "wherever he strode." "Randy" says: *"I don't have a steady girl-friend – they all wriggle around a bit."*

The Prince has followed the Royal and ancient tradition of skulking off to join the armed forces, rather than getting a job. *"The Navy's taught me a lot,"* he says. *"They've taught me that they deal with the 'boat' side of things, and mostly do stuff in water."*

He lists his hobbies as *"Burying the Family Jewels"*, *"Clam diving"*, and *"Wiggling the Warrior"*.

SAUSAGE OF THE MONTH: *The Cumberland Spicy*

HIS FAVOURITE THINGS:

Favourite Book: *"My favourite book is the bottom of page 60 of 'Lolita' by a Russian guy."*

Favourite grammatical construction: *"The obsolete pronoun* 'one' *used often and inappropriately."*

Favourite drink: *"Long Slow Comfortable Screw, and a glass of milk."*

Favourite saying: *"Oh, yes, that's so good, oh yes."*

Top: *Our Falklands hero carries some reminders of his victories.*
Right: *Two of the world's greatest photographers are about to meet Lichfield and Andy.*

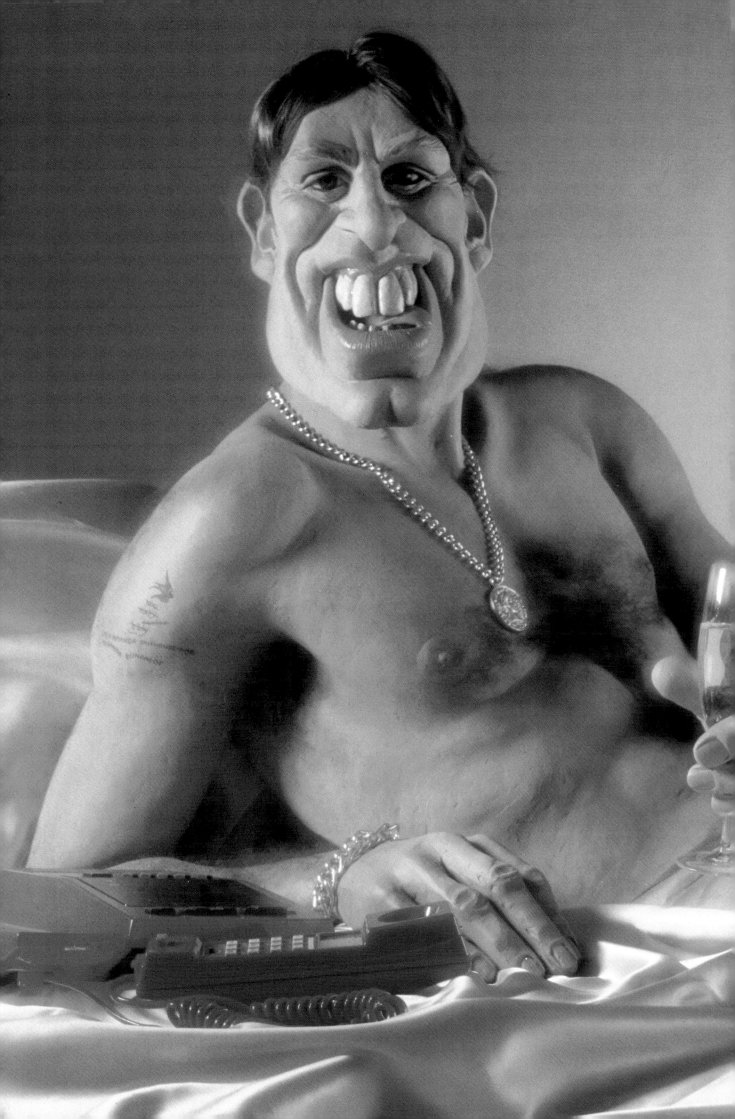

CECIL PARKINSON ➤

"I've been celibate ever since I was caught on the job. And it makes for deeper more caring relationships, and of course, you get your own cabinet post back again."

the new celibates

(MS. SHIELDS' BOOK IS SERIALISED ON PAGE 95)

● VICKIE HODGE

"I think celibacy's a great idea. Maybe I'll try it one evening next week. That is, unless *you're* free. Oh well, another time perhaps."

● BROOKE SHIELDS

"I'm a virgin and proud of it – I'm waiting for Mr. Right to come along. And when he does, obviously I'm going to be bonked senseless. I mean wham, bam, a tissue ma'am. But until that magical moment, I'm quite prepared to make an *absolute fortune* out of this new Celibacy thing."

EVERYONE is not doing it! So what's so great about sex anyway? That's what a generation of new young clean-living celibates are saying. *"It's a sort of ... reaction to the promiscuity ... of the Sixties"* says one young person I've just made up. One of the countless tens of people who are jumping on the bandwagon, and not on each other. The lead, as ever comes from the rich and famous.

◉ BOY GEORGE

"I prefer a hot cup of tea. But it doesn't half make your willie sore."

● VICTORIA GILLICK

"I'm firmly in favour of it. For me, my husband and my ten children."

MICHAEL JACKSON ➤

"I'll have sex when I feel the time is right. When I meet the right girl, get married, and when my voice breaks and my balls drop."

◉ PRINCE CHARLES

"Oh, you mean *not* playing 'Mr. Wobbly Hides His Helmet'? Oh. Why not? It's fun. I've done it twice now. Found I enjoyed it tremendously. I'm thinking of going for the hat-trick."

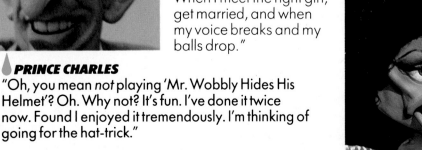

Well, there you have it. Or rather don't have it. Like it or lump it, sex is here to stay or not, as the case may be. Say what you like, the young people of today ... Oh sod it – I can't write any more of this garbage. I'm going out to get laid.

i Fans,

    Paul here. How are you? Many people ask me — how do I write such great lyrics? Where do I get all those magical words from? Those magical rhymes? And of course, those . . . magical images.

Well, basically, it's not something you can pin down. Without wishing to sound pretentious — it's very difficult for a genius to explain his craft. It's just something that happens — and it can happen at any time.

At a desk, sitting in bed with a pad of paper and a pen, in front of a typewriter. Anywhere! And you've got to be ready to grasp the iron while it's nettled — because these moments often pass, and the moment is lost. However, there are certain tips which can be learnt — which, if you like, can be supplemented to and complementary with your basic intangible talent.

Here are some lyrics sent to me by a budding young lyricist. I have appended my comments (in the red ink) — see if you think they help.

✦ ✦ ✦

Hi again, Fans. Basically, a fine lyric. I see what our friend is trying to say. Some of the imagery is devastating, and the chorus says it all — although, as I stated, there are probably 46 "Oh yeah's" too many. I would rework this — but do not give up whatever you do.

This is a potential No. 1 lyric, and I'm not just saying that. If you've got talent, don't hide it.

That's what I say.

All the best, Fans. See you soon.

Paul X.

[handwritten annotations on lyric sheet:]

Good rhyme with 'couch' Unfortunately should be at the end of the line for maximum effect. However if 'couch' in line 2 is replaced by 'bed' — you're in the shit. Perhaps you should replace 'head' in line 1 with something that rhymes with 'couch' and 'ouch'. 'Pouch'?

The sun is shining in my head
and I am lying on my couch
Someone hits me on the nose
Ouch I cry, that was sore

BAD. DOESN'T RHYME Just a thought but you may find bed would be a suitable replacement word here

Oh yeah, Oh yeah, Oh yeah
Oh yeah, Oh yeah, Oh yeah
Oh yeah, Oh yeah, Oh yeah
Oh yeah, Oh yeah, Oh yeah
Oh yeah, Oh yeah, Oh yeah

GOOD

Impressive Vocabulary. There is a suspicion I'm afraid that you have simply leafed thru the 'M' section of a dictionary

Mash, Mashie, Mask, Mask
Maskar, Maskinonge, Masochism
Mason, Mason-Dixon, Masonry
Masorah, Masorete, Masque

try to keep under the 100 mark.

You could always break it up a bit by spelling 'Yeah' as 'Yeh' on occasion. I think it would help.

Oh yeah, Oh yeah, Oh yeah X 146

My pink toothbrush melts in the purple sun and seven chocolate horsemen get a plastic parking ticket

WOW!!

Oh yeah, Oh yeah, Oh yeah.....
(Fade)

Good idea.

WHEN WHITEHALL TAKES OVER LONDON THERE WON'T BE ANY MORE OF THESE BLOODY POSTERS.

GLC WASTING YOUR MONEY

MOZART WRITES AGAIN?

"Mozart is writing through me – and it's a curse!" claims Spiritualist and former George Formby impersonator, Colin Jugg.

On September 17th, 1979, at 4.30 a.m., Colin awoke to find what he describes as: "a Mozarty presence" in his room. Whereupon the Mozart-like apparition walked through the wall, came back, apologised and walked through the door.

Three nights later, Mozart returned.

"He seemed very sad and embittered. Especially about Waldo de los Rios getting into the charts with a disco version of his 40th Symphony. So, with his hand guiding mine, I started to write new concertos and the occasional crossword, for light relief."

AN EXPERT'S OPINION:
"Undeniably Mozarty in approach."
ANOTHER EXPERT'S OPINION:
"This is the hand of the master all right."
MIKE READ'S OPINION:
"I'm sorry I haven't got one."

SPONTANEOUS COMBUSTION
AN EMBARRASSING PROBLEM

Anyone can suffer from spontaneous combustion. And boy, is it embarrassing. At a dinner party, at the office, massaging your grand mother – and blam! you explode into plumes of towering flames.

So why not try **Anderson's new asbestos underpants?** They're comfortable, they don't flake much and they keep the fire down to manageable proportions.

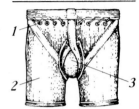

1. SMOKE-ACTIVATED SPRINKLER SYSTEM
2. SNUG ALUMINIUM COATING
3. EMERGENCY ESCAPE HATCH

HUNDREDS OF SATISFIED POTENTIAL VICTIMS

"I've been wearing **Anderson's** underpants for three years – and I haven't exploded once" (E.R. – London)

"I've been wearing **Anderson's** underpants for eight years – and I'm thinking of buying a second pair" (Paula Yates – London)

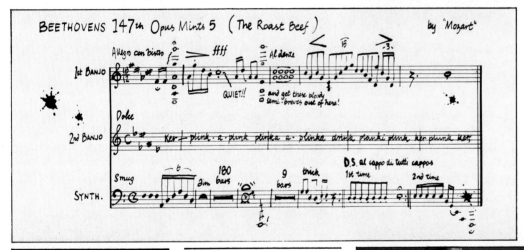

STRANGE THINGIES EXPERIMENT

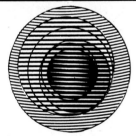

Study this shape without blinking for three hours, then shave – What do you look like?

ANSWER: ONE OF THE CYBER-MEN FROM "DOCTOR WHO".

NEXT WEEK'S ISSUE

OUT OF THE BODY EXPERIENCE – A Weekend at a Real Ale Festival

FROG RAIN – Just after I'd washed my car. (*Photo Feature*)

DOES GOD EXIST – Or is life meaningless?

THE AZTECS – A look at the civilisation so advanced, it was once honoured with its own chocolate bar.

DON'T MISS NEXT WEEK'S ISSUE! PLACE A COPY WITH YOUR NEWSAGENT *NOW!* and see where it gets you.

HERE'S A STRANGE THING Cats can actually "smell" colours. Sadly, there is no way of proving this.

FANTASTIC BINDER OFFER!!!!

Now you can cherish your STRANGE THINGIES magazine collection by sending off for this wondrously magnificent awe-inspiring calf leather binder, with gold leaf trim, diamond encrusted inlay, and sort of stringy elastic things with glue on them in the middle.

Week by week, issue by issue your STRANGE THINGIES collection builds and builds, until we go bankrupt after issue three. Now you can lovingly preserve each perfectly-formed edition which will give you minutes and minutes of reading pleasure for only a great deal of money indeed.

Please completely destroy this magazine you so desperately want to preserve for time immemorial by cutting along the dotted line and posting it to STRANGE THINGIES UNSOLVED UNEXPLAINED WAR MACHINE unique binder offer.

Name _____

Address _____

AND DON'T DELAY – THIS OFFER ONLY LASTS UNTIL WE GET KICKED OUT OF OUR OFFICES.

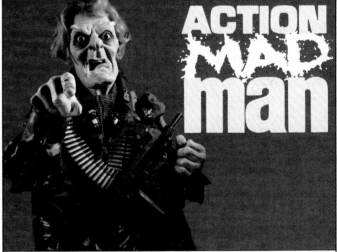

The dead of night – February 1985 – under cover of darkness "Mad" Mike H storms in with submachine gun coughing death – will he win? Well – it's up to you.

PONCY HAIRSTYLE
TOUGH LOBOTOMY SCAR
AUTHENTIC ROLLING EYES
FOAMING SALIVA
NO EMBARRASSING GENITALIA
PALM HAIR

Yes – re-enact the Battle of Molesworth with Mike Heseltine – **ACTION MADMAN** (TM) – in one of his super outfits:
★ FLAK JACKET ★
★ DINNER JACKET ★
★ STRAIT JACKET ★

Pit him against his deadly enemies DIRTY HIPPY MAN (TM) with realistic flares and unwashable underpants with realistic joints. And FILTHY LESBIAN MAN (TM) with drawstring dungarees, papoose and GRUBBY BABY (TM)

ACCESSORIES:
★ SHREDDER (DOUBLES AS TOASTER) ★ AUTHENTIC SECRET TO LOSE OR GIVE AWAY TO DEADLY ENEMIES ★ SPECIAL GOVT. ISSUE SUNGLASSES TO PROTECT AGAINST ATOM BOMBS ★ HIPPY KILLING PANZER ★ PADDED BOX TO KEEP HIM IN

I MADE LOVE TO AN ALIEN

He wanted me to have his Star child

"The most amazing day of my life began one hot summer morning in the middle of July. As an ex-beauty queen, I'd always been proud of my 44-23-34 figure – but I little dreamed my voluptuous form would single me out for an alien lover.

I was sunbathing in a skimpy bikini when my 14-year old cousin, Sheldon, who was staying with us that summer, came up to me. I had never liked him. He had terrible acne, and a horrible way of staring at me. Breathlessly he told me the news – an alien saucer had landed, and its occupant wanted to meet me in the garage in five minutes."

PASSION

"I arrived at the rendez vous expecting to be disappointed. How wrong I was. A few minutes later, the Starman appeared before me. He was about the height of a teenage boy, but his head was shaped like a cardboard box, and he sported a winceyette cape, and some red wellington-like boots.

"Undress," he rasped, "I wish to spread my star-spawn." Nervously, I complied with his orders. Staring at my naked form, the Starman began to unbuckle his inter-galactic corduroy trousers. "Thank you, Jesus" he cried in his low monotone.

LESS THAN A MINUTE

We committed the act of "Thringorrr", which is very much like Earth love-making, only shorter.

That whole summer was one of the happiest of my life, as my Starman chose me above all the other Earth women for what he called: "serious poking over a long period of time".

"Undress" he rasped,
I wish to spread my Star-spawn."

NEXT WEEK: "My acne-ridden star child"

PYRAMIDOLOGY
by Prof. G. Wagstaffe

What is it about the pyramid shape that has life-preserving qualities? A tomato, placed under a pyramid shape will stay fresh for longer than a tomato kept in a fridge. I spent 3 weeks living under a lead pyramid, and now, amazingly enough, I look like a tomato.

HOW WERE THE PYRAMIDS MADE?

Q: How was it possible for the Ancient Egyptians to perform these feats of architectural, mathematical and engineering skill? Moving countless tons of stone across impossible distances, and raising them to impossible heights?

A: Whips.

HERE'S A STRANGE THING   The average IQ of people who like Paul Hardcastle records is 19.

STRANGE
THINGIES

ISSUE 1 £1.00

the magazine that investigates spookines

WAS GOD AN ASTRONAUT?
And if so – does he have a crew cut?

CHAPPAQQUIDDICK –
Will we ever know the true spelling?

The Marie Celeste –
Was it a business lunch for Ken Dodd and Jimmy Mulville?

The Greatest Mystery of All
Why do mags like this inexplicably vanish from the news stands after only two issues?
And why do they always give away issue two free with issue one?

TUTANKHAMEN'S CURSE –
Why did the boy king have periods?

The Lost City of Atlantis –
is it down *your* settee?

Reincarnation –
Why does Gary Glitter keep coming back as the same thing?

The Blurry Monster of Nepal
Photographic evidence. See P.12

FREE INSIDE – ISSUE TWO!!!

ENGLISH LANGUAGE EDITION
(SORRY ABOUT THE TYPING)

WOW! JUST LOOK AT THAT ECONOMY GO!

SILENCE FOR THE COURAGEOUS STRIKE OF THE CAVIARE MINERS, 1983!

PRAVDA

A Rupert Murdoch/News International Publication

CIRCULATION: 225,000,000
Still cheaper than our rivals: The Blanket, The Firelighter, and the Thermal Pantaloon

OFFICIAL PRICE; 4 KOPEKS   TWELFTHDAY, 46TH BERIA 1985   BLACK MARKET PRICE: ⅓ KOPEK

CRAZY PRAVDA BINGO
WIN A MILLION

HOW TO LIE IN STATE

I JOINED THE "LYING IN STATE" DEPARTMENT IN MOSCOW IN THE LATE 50'S. OF COURSE, THEN I WAS ONLY A JUNIOR. THE FIRST BODY I DEALT WITH WAS KRUSCHEV'S. OF COURSE – BEING ONLY A JUNIOR – MY INVOLVEMENT WAS MINIMAL. MY BRIEF WAS KRUSCHEV'S TOES – WITH PARTICULAR REFERENCE TO KEEPING THEM CONCEALED. IT MAY NOT SOUND TERRIBLY DIFFICULT – BUT IN FACT KRUSCHEV'S TOES PROVED TO BE ONE OF THE MOST DIFFICULT AREAS. YOU SEE, THEY WERE THE LAST PART OF HIM TO DIE. THE NIGHT BEFORE WE LAID HIM OUT EVERYTHING WAS SET WITH JUST THE UPPER PART OF THE LEADER'S BODY ON SHOW. FOR MY PART – THE GREAT MAN'S TOES WERE SUCCESSFULLY HIDDEN AWAY BENEATH THE FLAG. HOWEVER – IMAGINE MY HORROR WHEN THE NEXT MORNING WE FOUND THOSE DEVOTED LITTLE MEMBERS DEFIANTLY STANDING TO ATTENTION FOR ALL TO SEE. I WAS DEVASTATED. THANKFULLY BASTARDOV WHO WAS IN CHARGE WAS VERY UNDERSTANDING. I REMEMBER HE CALLED ME OVER AND SAID IN A QUIET VOICE "VALERI – IF YOU DON'T HIDE THOSE TOES IMMEDIATELY – I'LL SEND YOU TO SIBERIA YOU LITTLE NAMESAKE." IN THE EVENT – NOBODY NOTICED THAT COMRADE KRUSCHEV'S TOES WERE POKING OUT OF HIS BREAST POCKET.

AFTER THIS BRESHNEV CAME TO POWER. AS HE REMAINED IN OFFICE FOR 20 YEARS THERE WAS LITTLE FOR US TO DO DURING THIS PERIOD. OBVIOUSLY – WE HAD TO CLEAR UP THE KRUSCHEV MESS – BUT THAT ONLY TOOK US UP TO LUNCHTIME ON THE DAY BRESHNEV TOOK OVER.

THERE WERE LIGHT MOMENTS AS WELL – PARTICULARLY WHEN COMRADE BASTARDOV DIED IN 1970. CHERNENKO PROVIDED US WITH NUMEROUS NEW DIFFICULTIES. 6 TIMES WE HAD HIM EMBALMED DURING HIS SHORT PERIOD IN POWER AND SIX TIMES HE GOT UP AND WALKED AWAY AFTERWARDS. HE WAS VERY GOOD ABOUT IT THOUGH. HE JUST USED TO SAY "SORRY, LADS – I THINK I'M STILL ALIVE. I'LL KEEP IN TOUCH," AND OFF HE WOULD GO. NUMEROUS TIMES HE APPEARED IN MY OFFICE – CASUALLY STATING "I'M DEAD, VALERI – LET'S GET ON WITH IT" – ONLY TO RECOVER LATER. WHEN WE FINALLY GOT HIM – WE NAILED HIM DOWN.

THE NEW MAN GORBACHEV LOOKS LIKE A BIT OF A STAYER. NO BAD THING REALLY. THE DEPARTMENT NEEDS A BREAK.

AND WHAT OF ME – HEAD OF THE DEPARTMENT SINCE 1970. PEOPLE SUGGEST I RETIRE – BUT WHAT WOULD I DO. I THINK I'LL PROBABLY STAY HERE UNTIL MY DEATH – AND PROBABLY FOR 4 OR 5 YEARS AFTER THAT. THEN I MIGHT CONSIDER TAKING THINGS A BIT EASIER.

SALES FEVER HITS MOSCOW

INTREPID SHOPPERS WITH AN EYE FOR A BARGAIN ARE ALREADY QUEUING FOR THE JANUARY SALES – RIGHT NOW IN FEBRUARY! MRS. BORODIN, OF STATE APARTMENT 33345774b HAS GOT HER SIGHTS FIXED ON A LOAF OF BREAD!

"I'VE SEEN IT THERE FOR MONTHS, AND I REALLY WANT IT" SHE CHIRPED. OTHER EXCITED SHOPPERS ARE HOPING TO SNAP UP A PIECE OF MEAT AT THE GIVEAWAY PRICE OF 50,000 ROUBLES.

BUT SURELY THE MOST THRILLING BARGAIN ON OFFER IS DISPLAYED PROMINENTLY IN THE EMPTY WINDOW OF THE GUM DEPARTMENT STORE. A FABULOUS MATCHING PAIR OF SHOES, SIZE THREE.

BUT PROSPECTIVE SHOPPERS ARE WARNED NOT TO BE DISAPPOINTED, BECAUSE THE QUEUE ALREADY STRETCHES TWICE ROUND LENIN'S TOMB AND ALL THE WAY TO OMSK.

PRAVDA POP CHARTS
(LAST YEAR'S FIGURES IN BRACKETS)

(1) 1 THUNDERBIRDS ARE GO! (Theme)
G & S ANDERSON

(2) 2 These boots Are Made For Walkin'
NANCY SINATRA

(3) 3 Swingin' Safari
BERT KAMPFERT AND HIS ORCHESTRA

(4) 4 bits 'n' Pieces
DAVE CLARKE FIVE

(5) 5 Now That's What I Call Solemn Music!
VARIOUS

TV LISTINGS

CHANNEL ONE
1.00 SOLEMN MUSIC
2.00 SOLEMN MUSIC
3.00 ANNOUNCEMENT OF DEATH
4.00 SOLEMN MUSIC
5.00 WOGAN
6.00 SOLEMN MUSIC (RPT)
7.00 ANNOUNCEMENT OF DEATH

LAST NIGHT'S VIEW
SO THAT'S WHAT CHANNEL ONE CALL "SOLEMN MUSIC" IS IT? NOT IN MY BOOK, IT AIN'T! FRANKLY, I'VE HEARD MORE SOLEMN MUSIC AT A BEER FESTIVAL IN THE UKRAINE. COME OFF IT, CHANNEL ONE— LET'S HAVE SOME REAL SOLEMN MUSIC HUH?

THE LOVELIEST SHOT-PUTTERS ARE ALL IN YOUR PRAVDA

PRAVDA PUTTER LOVELY SAMANTHA FOXOV IS REALLY GOOD AT HANDLING BIG BALLS. IN FACT SHE THREW THEM 175 METRES AT THE CZECHOSLOVAK OLYMPIC GAMES LAST SUMMER! SUPER SAM SAYS: "WE SHOT PUTTERS ARE NOT JUST PRETTY FACES." AND SHE SHOULD KNOW, BECAUSE THE MOSCOW BEAUTY SPENT FIVE YEARS STUDYING AT THE GORKY INSTITUTE FOR ADVANCED COMBINE HARVESTER SERVICING. SO SHE'S NOT AS THICK AS SHIT AFTER ALL!

IN OUR ONE MILLION POTATO BINGO

IMAGINE YOUR OWN DREAM HOME, BUILT OF POTATOES. A ROUND-THE-WORLD-CRUISE ON A LUXURY POTATO RAFT.

WELL – MAYBE NOT – BUT YOU CAN EAT THEM. WE'VE ALREADY GIVEN AWAY ONE MILLION POTATOES THIS YEAR – AND THERE ARE MORE WHERE THAT CAME FROM (SUBJECT TO AVAILABILITY).

OUR POTATO MILLIONAIRE, IRINA KASPOV SAYS:

"I NEVER DREAMT I'D END UP WITH A MILLION POTATOES.
IN INTEREST ALONE I EARN 800 POTATOES A DAY."

WE ASKED FOR YOUR AMUSING STORIES ABOUT TRACTORS. HERE'S A SELECTION OF THE BEST . . .

I WAS OUT IN THE FIELD ON THE COLLECTIVE FARM WHEN MY TRACTOR BROKE DOWN, OR SO I THOUGHT! HOW WRONG I WAS! RUSSIAN TRACTORS NEVER BREAK DOWN, AS I LEARNED DURING MY THREE YEARS AT THE REHABILITATION CENTRE. WE LAUGHED AND LAUGHED AS WE PLOUGHED THE FIELDS WITH OUR BARE HANDS!
M. GOLCHIK

WE PLAYED A MARVELLOUS JOKE ON OUR FOREMAN HERE AT THE LENINGRAD TRACTOR FACTORY. WE TOLD HIM PRODUCTION HAD RISEN TO AN ASTONISHING 15 MILLION TRACTOR UNITS PER HOUR PER MAN. IT HADN'T OF COURSE. IT HAD ACTUALLY RISEN TO 234 MILLION TRACTORS PER MINUTE PER MAN. I STILL LAUGH TO THINK ABOUT IT!
MRS. KONRANDSKI.

THE THINGS THEY SAY:
I WAS IN THE KITCHEN STUDYING THE LATEST PRODUCTION FIGURES, WHEN MY FIVE-YEAR-OLD SON CAME IN AND SAID: "YOU ARE HARBOURING ANTI-SOVIET THOUGHTS. I BELIEVE YOU ARE A REVISIONIST, AND I HAVE REPORTED YOU TO THE KGB. HOW WE LAUGHED AS THEY DROVE US AWAY.
MRS. GULPOV, LUBYANKA.

PRAVDA SAYS CRIKEY!

WHAT KIND OF WORLD ARE WE LIVING IN? EH? WHEN THE PRESIDENT OF THE UNITED STATES INTRODUCES A MISSILE WHICH EATS THE FIRST-BORN CHILD OF EVERY SOVIET CITIZEN. WELL, WE'VE SAID IT BEFORE, AND WE'LL SAY IT AGAIN:
SOD OFF RONNIE!!!
AND TAKE YOUR IMPERIALIST CAPITALIST RUNNING DOGS WITH YOU!

GORBACHOV STILL ALIVE SHOCK (SEE PAGE FIVE)

This book belongs to

_____

_____

So sod off and get your own copy

YOUR EDITORIAL TEAM

David Stoten, 20. Gifted young *Spitting Image* caricaturist. His uncanny abilities may be glimpsed in the brilliant models of Tim Watts.

Stephen Bendelack, 22. Luck and Flaw's likeable, dedicated young assistant. It is he who paints all the puppets using a selection of fumes, acids and diseases.

Alex Evans, 26. Distinctive, individualistic, brilliant young art director of the *Spitting Image* book.

Lord Lucan 48. Associate Producer. Since joining the *Spitting Image* team Lord has fitted in tremendously well, and has been invaluable in murdering any 'dead wood' on the production.

Moray Hunter, 50. Writer. Current project: working on biographical details for the *Spitting Image* book.

...out, ...Moray, I'll ...nip down ...to Woolies ...and sort out the passport photos.

Tim Watts, 17. Brilliant, individualistic, distinctive young *Spitting Image* caricaturist and bottom-sculptor.

John Docherty, 19. Writer. You get the script roughed

sketches based?

It's a little-known fact, that *all* the puppets in *Spitting Image* are actually likenesses of real people. For example, Reagan's aide "Ed" is a caricature of a bloke called Ed Meese who happens to be the U.S. Attorney General. The bald woman who eats human flesh and has a willie is a faithful rendering of Mrs Margaret Thatcher, the Prime Minister of Britain.

But aside from the caricatures of the rich, famous and successful even the "nobodies" who sometimes appear in the background – as waitresses, taxi-drivers and members of the Labour Party, for instance – are modelled from life.

Such "faceless" puppets are based on the numerous deformed social misfits who huddle around the *Spitting Image* office as if for money: the floor-sweepers, toilet-cleaners, office-prostitutes, writers and so on.

For example:

Roger Law, 44. A giant barrel-cheeked ogre of a man with eyes like blood-oranges and fists like two clenched leather potting-sheds, he nurses a fierce hatred of the system that forced him to leave school at 4½ after he ate it.

Peter Fluck, 44. A quiet, gentle, easy-going old gentleman who has sworn never to kill another living

thing unless it irritates him in some way.

John Lloyd, 103. Formerly known as 'Tony Hendra', he has since retired to the BBC where he was born, and now whiles away the autumn of his years pruning his beloved old peak-time sitcoms.

Rob Grant, 29. Dashing, fashion-conscious, tough young script-editor.

Non-sexist, non-racist, non-ageist: anything with an orifice that goes moist at the sight of a demob suit welcome. BOX 267. A.L.A.

...going, ...mate? Drink?

Doug Naylor, 29. Handsome, charming twinkle-toothed young script editor and sexual beast. Solvent, magnificently-hung, own Lancia.

Ian Hislop, 12. Writer. Deputy Editor of *Private Eye*. Very nice fellow. Hallo, Ian mate, have some more money. Great scripts, mate. Crawl fawn cringe.

Geoff Atkinson, 25. Writer. Average scriptfall 250 tonnes per hr. Married with four word-processors.

Nick Newman, 23. Talented young writer and cartoonist. Friend of Ian Hislop and who can blame him. Hi there, Ian. How's it

Illustration
Ian Dicks: *Heineken*.
Mike Terry: *Kentucky Chicken, Obvious Fish, Swissarmyknifeosaur*.
Cooper West: *Tory Map, Goalkeeping, Bum Pat, On The Beat*.
Phil Green: *Spanish Airport*.
Tom Lubbock: *Neo Narcissism*.
Roger Payne: *Masquerade*.
Paul Sample: *Custom Hair*.
Eric Beaumont: *Starchild*.

Special photography
John Lawrence-Jones: *Front and back covers, Cosmopolitan, TV Times, Cringing Royalist, A La Carte, Masquerade, Nouvelle Cuisine, The Lady, Hot Dog, No FT..., Action Madman*.
Mike Prior: *Photo Story, Campain, Loan Ranger*.
Pat Oleszko Sew What: *Strange Thingies*.
John Melville: *Table Swimming, Sand Worms, Durham Bible*.
Mark Westwood: *Mars Bar, Action Madman*.

Photographic Sources: Allsport, Photo Source, Press Association.

Typesetting: Signal 'Huge Wodge' Communications.

Additional Jokes: Peter Brewis, Tony Sarchet, Andrea Solomons, Nick George.

Company Secretary: The hard done by Anne Newcombe

Research: David Bond.

Transport: Smart Cars.

Workshop Assistant: Julian Short

General Assistant: Alice Cooper.

Workshop Artist: Scott Brooker
Special thanks to *Western Styling* for the Loan Ranger's clothes.

This book was assembled at **Millions Design** by the brilliant likeable and young Nigel Soper, Philip 'Strange Thingie' Chidlow, Allan 'Hopefully' Mole, Liz 'Hot Dog' Barnett, Karen 'Midnight' Byrne, Fifi 'the Lone Bagel', Clive 'Lines' Frampton, Stefan 'Tonto' Morris, John 'Red' Bradley, Chris Krage, and Tim Shussy to the tunes of Xavier Cugat and the Cyril Stapleton Orchestra.

THE APPALLINGLY DISRESPECTFUL SPITTING IMAGE BOOK

This edition published 1985 by Book Club Associates by arrangement with Faber and Faber Limited Printed in Great Britain

All rights reserved

© 1985 Spitting Image Productions Ltd.

This book is sold subject to the condition that it shall not, by way of trade or otherwise, be lent, resold, hired out or otherwise circulated without the publisher's prior consent in any form of binding or cover other than that in which it is published and without a similar condition including this condition being imposed on the subsequent purchaser blah blah blah blah blah blah blah blah blah blah blah

British Library Cataloguing in Publication Data.

Lloyd, John
    Spitting Image.
    I. Title
    828'.91409   PR6062.L6/

ISBN 0-571-13670-2